Re-understanding the Child's Right to Identity

Nijhoff Law Specials

VOLUME 92

The titles published in this series are listed at *brill.com/nlsp*

Re-understanding the Child's Right to Identity

On Belonging, Responsiveness and Hope

By

Ya'ir Ronen

BRILL
NIJHOFF

LEIDEN | BOSTON

Library of Congress Cataloging-in-Publication Data

Names: Ronen, Ya'ir
Title: Re-understanding the child's right to identity : on belonging, responsiveness and hope / by Ya'ir Ronen.
Description: Leiden : Brill, 2016. | Series: Nijhoff law specials ; 92 | Includes bibliographical references and index.
Identifiers: LCCN 2016016071 (print) | LCCN 2016016154 (ebook) | ISBN 9789004223660 (pbk. : alk. paper) | ISBN 9789004223677 (E-book)
Subjects: LCSH: Children's rights. | Children--Legal status, laws, etc. | Identity (Philosophical concept).
Classification: LCC K639 .R655 2016 (print) | LCC K639 (ebook) | DDC 342.08/772--dc23
LC record available at https://lccn.loc.gov/2016016071

Typeface for the Latin, Greek, and Cyrillic scripts: "Brill". See and download: brill.com/brill-typeface.

ISSN 0924-4549
ISBN 978-90-04-22366-0 (paperback)
ISBN 978-90-04-22367-7 (e-book)

This book is printed on acid-free paper and produced in a sustainable manner.

מוקדש באהבה לעילוי נשמת רחל סעדי בת סנמבר ורחמים חכימיאן בן מלכה

דרך התוודעותי להתמודדויות השונות שלהם למדתי להכיר בערכם של שונות אנושית והיענות לאחר

Dedicated lovingly to the memory of my grandmother Rachel Sa'adi and my grandfather Rachamim Chakimyan

Through witnessing their different struggles I learnt the value of human diversity and responsiveness to the Other

Contents

Foreword

Much has been written on the right to identity. The question arises across a range of problem areas, which with the so- called reproduction revolution are increasing all the time. Life – certainly identity – was easier when the birth of a child required a sexual congress between a man and a woman, before IVF, PGD, surrogacy had entered the imagination, before the French invented accouchement sous x, before uterus and penis transplants, before it was possible to have more than two parents, And there is more to puzzle yet to come. We are promised exogenesis, and threatened with male pregnancy. And we thought grappling with adoption was difficult! It is not surprising that when the Bible wanted to explain wisdom, it told us a tale which required King Solomon to identify the true mother. This story is told and retold today in plays like Brecht's *Caucasian Chalk Circle* and in courts across the world. What is a court to do when a fertility clinic fertilizes a woman's ovum with the wrong sperm? This happened in Leeds in England in 2003, but we only know about it because the woman was white and the man black. It is not difficult to speculate how often accidents like this have passed unnoticed, how often a woman has taken the wrong baby home from the maternity ward. At least today, we have DNA testing.

The right to identity is raised in a multitude of contexts, often contested and some novel. An example of a new problem area is the practice of male circumcision. Not since the Emperor Hadrian had authority challenged it until it came under attack in Scandinavia and then in Germany [of all places] and The Netherlands in the last few years. Analogies were drawn with female genital mutilation, rightly censored from the 1980s. In both, there is a conflict of two interests – identity and bodily integrity. But given the minimal harm that male circumcision causes as against the long-term deleterious consequences of FGM, any equation of the two practices is facile. It is easy to see that cultural and religious identity trumps momentary pain, but succumbs to permanent disabilities. But many do not see this and tell us the boy has not consented. Good Christian families, of course seek the consent of their children before having them baptized!

Children down the ages have dreamt that someone else is their parent. The revelation that you are not who you thought you were is central to the plots of operas as diverse as *Le Nozze di Figaro, La Juive, Il Trovatore* and *The Pirates of Penzance,* and countless others. And where would Shakespeare's comedies be without some identity crisis or other? "Identity" has now become a subject for peak time television with programs delving into the past to uncover who you think you are.

Of course, we all have an interest in our identity. We do not want to make the same mistakes as Oedipus! But what kind of an interest is it? There are at least three possibilities. There is a desire to know one's origins. There is a need to know one's medical history, so as to avoid the possibility of marriage within the prohibited degrees of consanguinity, with all the problems attendant upon this. There is the benefit of being qualified to take property in the event of the death of a social parent – a material interest. Of the three, it is the first which tends to assume greatest significance today, though the second will have increasing importance in the future. Without a knowledge of one's origins we are deracinated. We may suffer, what has been called "genealogical bewilderment."

This book offers a refreshing new take on identity, and in the process much else besides. We hear much less today of therapeutic jurisprudence than was once the case, rather more of the philosophy of Emmanuel Levinas, almost a cult figure now, than we did a decade ago. And the more one reads Levinas, the more enlightening and path-breaking his writings appear. Ronen offers some valuable insight into his scholarship.

This is an original and thought-provoking book, building on experience and interdisciplinary research. It sheds light on the identity debate and on many other issues.

Professor M.D.A. Freeman, UCL.

Prologue

This book signals a closure for a facet of my academic work on identity that sprung out of a doctorate in law I submitted in 2001.

However, my fascination with these issues started much earlier than 2001, when I first came out with written work on the subject. My writing is the end result of a process which started decades earlier.

Should I share with you here what brought me to write this book?

I believe I should.

When I started studying law in 1986, there was much less scholarly interest in what brought us to explore the issues we study. I felt that much of the time, we were taught in law school implicitly and explicitly that justice is blind – or should be blind. We were subtly invited to blind ourselves to the personal narratives from which our sense of justice grew. Something inside me always rebelled against this message, I never internalized it as part of my identity as a scholar. The intellectual climate has changed. I am happy that our understanding of scholarly work is evolving and that we are becoming more open to learn about the personal narratives and value-laden choices that play a role in our writing. At the end of the day, original scholarly writing is a form of creative writing. Law concerns justice and therefore recognizing our inevitable subjectivity is alarming, anxiety provoking and invites objections. Nevertheless, the author as a whole person is present today more than ever before even in legal writing.

I believe it is methodologically important and ethically right to come out with a personal statement starting to share the place I come from when writing a book such as this one. Through this effort, I endeavor to make a small contribution to the ongoing transformation of what is considered scholarly, making the personal even more present, recognizable and valuable. Indeed, the personal is political but that does not make it less truly personal, unique and diversified.

As a Jew of Iranian descent born in Israel in the 1960s I had to come to terms with my feeling and thoughts about my cultural heritage in a predominantly Eurocentric culture. One day, one of my high school teachers complimented me on not looking Iranian. There was inner turmoil inside me. I said nothing to the teacher but I decided to reject the compliment, despite its alluring power in a culture which undervalued my origins. I started speaking Persian publically more and more with my grandparents and others. This is just one anecdote taken out of rich memories which brought me to explore the tie between children's dignity and their evolving self-constructed identity.

Feeling a strong affinity to Anglo Jewry as a child between the ages of ten and thirteen, when living in England, I discovered gentleness and humanity in a community coping meekly and sometimes timidly with Anti-Semitism. As time passes, I grow to be both more and more proud of the gentleness and humanity I experienced – and internalized – there. At the same time, I grow to be more critical of the typical non-assertive stance I witnessed there in response to affronts to Jewish identity.

Having returned to my home in Israel at age thirteen, I am still deciphering what growing to be a Jewish man means. I live in a society responding to existential threats through a new responsibility for protecting Jewish life. In my family, I belong to a first generation born to national freedom, after millennia of abnormal existence as a people without a state, an army or a police force.

How has the heritage of the persecuted Jewish diaspora influenced my development and identity? What is the place my Jewish-Iranian heritage? My childhood sense of belonging to Anglo Jewry? My personal encounter with anti-Semitism? How has the humaneness and alienation I experienced from Jews and from non-Jews, from family and others who crossed my path influenced my evolving identity? How has belonging to different disempowered minorities influenced what I write about and what I write?

I think it is important to for me to raise these questions and share them with you even though I do not always know my answers to them. In my eyes, raising these questions is more important than offering my answers to them.

I do know the influences are there and I know that I have made personal choices – sometimes unpopular choices – to accept and reject aspects of different traditions I was exposed to.

Not accidently, I originally started to write about how a right to identity can protect a sense of belonging. I was exposed to individuals and establishments during my childhood and youth which paid no respect to a child's sense of belonging and yet saw themselves as dedicated to uniform standardized application of just rules. Thus, re-understanding the child's right to identity as a right to belonging is the subject of the first chapter in this book. In earlier papers I wrote of redefining the right. Through dialogues with colleagues and students I realized, it is important for me to highlight re-understanding the right more than legally redefining it. Re-understanding what needs to be protected is a solid basis for both social and legal change.

I learnt the healing power of responsiveness through wonderful people whom I also encountered through my childhood and youth. They could consider my perspective when deciding what is just in situations influencing my life and ambitions. Later, as a child advocate in the field and in academia I thoroughly enjoyed being responsive and doing something for *Tikkun*

Olam – the Jewish (Hebrew) term for mending our broken world. For me, mending our world starts not with the big theoretical geopolitical or abstract philosophical musings but with mending the lives of individual children, individual Others, which can touch me, if I allow them. So I believe that 'Responsiveness to children and law's healing power' is a good choice for the second chapter of this book. In it I offer a preliminary exploration of the potential to intertwine Levinasian thought with Therapeutic Jurisprudence in the context of responsiveness to children.

Being exposed to great diversity in childhood and youth made me conscious of how remembering is a dynamic process. I became aware that a child or adolescent can exercise real power through choosing what to remember and how to remember it. There are different family and cultural narratives. You have to choose between them and make your own tapestry even if you end up with a narrative similar to one that you heard. I still remember the hostile response of my teacher of Classical Studies in England when at the age of twelve I put my finger up and said that Roman culture was morally lacking in the cruel way it related to slaves, enemies and monotheists. Her facial gesture and distinct disapproval surprised me. It was a lesson for me. I could feel intensely the conflict between the lessons I internalized from a historic past and those of my teacher. We agreed on the facts, interpreted their meaning differently and my teacher resented that. She had the power because she was the teacher and I was a child and a minority child at that. Thus, in Chapter 3, I explore how constructing memory relates to responsiveness to children and a children's rights consciousness. We struggle over memory. If children's experiences remain invisible and unrecognized, than the prospect of children's rights rhetoric to influence children's day-to-day reality becomes dismal.

Going along further on this path, I explore how the child's right to be oneself is related to the need to be a spiritually authentic being. Do we genuinely respect children who are well fed, enjoy expensive health and educational services, but are cut off from their heritage? I remember a need to express myself as a spiritual being, as someone who has more than material needs, that has an aspiring mind and spiritual ambitions. I remember struggling to find a place for spirituality in challenging social environments blind to this need. And so the fourth chapter delves into the question of whether and how we can allow our children the right to be spiritually authentic beings when exposed to an achievement-driven materialistic culture.

The fifth chapter closes this book through exploring the courage to hope and how it relates to protecting the child's sense of belonging. We all yearn to belong and at the same time achieve a sense of self-worth. It is painful to be asked to give up one for the other. There were people who had faith in me and a courage to hope I would succeed in my path. In turn, I too had the exciting privilege of aiding children change the course of their lives, give them voice and power, through my hope and faith in them. This led to a great fascination with how this process works, with finding the theory behind the practice. One outcome of this fascination is before you in Chapter 5.

This is a scholarly book.

I hope that those of you looking for scholarly work will not be deterred by the personal facet of this prologue. I believe that being thoughtful about our writing must include being thoughtful about what brings us to write.

I also hope that those of you who, like me, see themselves on an endless personal journey of self-discovery will read on, that my promise of a scholarly book will not deter you.

It can be satisfying to understand our selves better. However, I believe we should aim even higher. Through exploring our unique experiences we can and should participate in the mending of our world, in *Tikkun Olam*.

One way we can make our personal journeys valuable for people everywhere is trying to learn general lessons from written texts. Interpreting these texts is inevitably enriched by our unique experiences and worldview though we can only start to fathom how we enrich our interpretation through who we are.

We can sometimes articulate our lessons and offer them to others as scholarly work. This is what I have attempted to do here.

Acknowledgements

Writing this book has been a long journey. Having completed the journey, it is my pleasure to thank those who have made it possible and assisted along the way. I ask forgiveness of those who I may have forgotten to mention here.

I thank Michael Freeman, Member of the British Academy, professor emeritus of University College London whose kind and generous spirit and faith in me have been an inspiration for decades. I am honored that he agreed to write a forward to this book.

Richard Isralowitz, professor of public policy at Ben Gurion University, allowed me to enjoy his rich experience as an academic author. He is a valued colleague and I treasure his wise advice.

I thank the department of social work at Ben-Gurion University in the Negev Israel, the university's rector, president and dean of the faculty of social sciences and humanities for their financial support to this project.

It was excellent working with Adva Assulin, a talented soulful social worker and my dedicated research assistant. I cherish her careful assistance in preparing the book for publication.

My wife Gila, my daughters Tay, Noa and Shir and Aryeh Diamant who for me is a part of my close family, all influenced my thoughts and feelings in significant ways. Close friends and co-workers and several students and individuals whom I coached and counseled confidentially have a place in my mind and heart and are have taught me important lessons I am only starting to be mindful of. I am grateful to them all.

I thank Bea Timmer and Lindy Melman of Brill Publishers for their patient and kind support. It has been a pleasure working with them.

I thank God for all allowing me to make it, at times, against all odds and for reaching this stage in my personal journey.

A Note on Style

Whenever I use a masculine (or feminine) pronoun I have both sexes in mind unless a different meaning is implied from the context.

Using alternatives such as 'he or she' makes my writing less forceful and natural.

In other ways too this book mirrors my personal style of writing.

Our style is part of our identity. May each of us feel free to style his writing authentically.

May a thousand flowers blossom.

Permissions

This book is partially based on previous publications of the author. Thus, permission was given for using those publications as detailed below:

- "An Essay on Child Protection, Hope and Realism," by Ya'ir Ronen and Moshe Klein. *Social Development Issues* 29. *Special Issue: Child Protection – Challenges Worldwide*. pp. 96–109. 2007. By Permission of the President of the International Consortium for Social Development.
- "On the Child's Need to be One's Self," by Ya'ir Ronen. *Symposium Issue: Belonging, Families and Family Law. Brigham Young University Journal of Public Law* 25. pp. 233–243. 2011. http://digitalcommons.law.byu.edu/jpl/. By permission of the Editor-in-Chief of BYU Journal of Public Law.
- "Redefining the Child's Right to Identity," by Ya'ir Ronen. *International Journal of Law, Policy and the Family* 18. pp. 147–177. 2004. www.oup.com. By permission of Oxford University Press.
- "The Construction of Memory through Law and Law's Responsiveness to Children," by Ya'ir Ronen. *Current Legal Issues* 9. *Special Issue: Law and Psychology*. Edited by Michael Freeman and Melinda Brooks. pp. 406–429. 2006. www.oup.com. By permission of Oxford University Press.

CHAPTER 1

Re-understanding the Right to Identity as a Right to Belonging

I Introduction

In this chapter, I maintain the state should have a positive duty to safeguard the child's right to identity as a right to protection of his meaningful ties. It suggests that these ties delineate the child's identity. These are primarily ties to the human world. However, they can also be ties to an animal- such as a dog or a horse, to an inanimate object- such as a book or a tree, or to a geographic place- such as a village or a physical home.

I open with an exposition of the main arguments and focus. This introduction is followed by a discussion of authenticity, of the child's legally neglected need for a meaningful existence and of culture as a context of personal meaning. This discussion forms the rationale for the proposed definition of the right to identity. A critical discussion of the right to identity in international law follows, clarifying and exemplifying the need to redefine the right in positive law. I then bring before the reader the essence of the judicial narratives of two children as told by the Lord Justices of the English Court of Appeal in two cases. These narratives exemplify some of the problems related to identity that I discuss throughout the chapter. The chapter turns to an analysis of the narratives presented and ends with a concluding note exploring the key implications of the proposed re-understanding of the right.

The main arguments of this chapter are:

1. The child's right to identity derivative of his human dignity should protect the development of an authentic self-actualizing individual who maintains psychological ties, primarily ties of interdependence to significant others. The state should protect a right to an individualized identity by seeking the child's wishes and feelings concerning his ties. In this way, I introduce a structured element of caution into child law policy and practice.
2. Protection of an individualized identity necessitates exploring culture as a context of personal meaning and is founded on empathic understanding of an individual child's experience. We cannot equate such respect with what is commonly perceived as cultural sensitivity.

 | DOI 10.1163/9789004223677_002

3. Consequently, preferential protection of the child's ties to a minority culture or to individuals affiliated to that culture is seen as violating the right to identity. Such preferential protection signifying a politicized selectivity of compassion is an inappropriate tool to correct or counteract prejudices against such a minority culture.
4. Neither the United Nations Convention on the Rights of the Child (hereafter: The Convention or the UN Convention) nor the European Convention for the Protection of Human Rights and Fundamental Freedoms (hereafter: the European Convention) explicitly uphold the right to identity as defined here.

   The child's right to guidance formulated in Article 5 of the Convention and his right to free expression and his right to participation formulated respectively in Articles 12 and 13 to the Convention, as interrelated, implicitly reaffirm the commitment of international law to a dynamic child-constructed identity.
5. Legal protection of the proposed right not only reflects and protects a social reality in which children's lives may be imbued with personal meaning. It also creates such a reality through law's transformative educational impact.

The focus of my discussion is not any national law but rather international instruments, primarily the Convention. Though not incorporated into statute law in most jurisdictions the Convention is the most authoritative and influential text on children's rights (Brighouse 2002). English Courts, like many other domestic courts worldwide, have recognized that domestic administrative and legal procedures absorb the Convention's expectations and therefore, its minimalist and sometimes implicit references to identity are seen as deserving primary attention. The European Convention, clearly bearing on the two cases discussed here, is also discussed.

Following cultural anthropologist, Clifford Geertz (1983, 218), positive law, such as these two Conventions and case law, which should be guided by their imperatives, is seen here not only as reflecting social norms but also as constructing them through the articulation and enforcement of legal norms. Thus, law may influence both individual and community identity (Lukinsky 1987; Post 1995) through its transformation of local cultures (An-Na'im 1994). Therefore, law is seen as a tool for the promotion of social change despite the fact that cultural values influence its implementation (Alston 1994, 23) and irrespective of the fact that lawmakers sometimes deny its social impact.

II The Rationale for Re-understanding the Right to Identity

1 *Facilitating the Development of an Authentic Self-Actualizing Individual*

Increasingly, the child is seen as a human being worthy of the protection of a human rights regime not only by international law but also by societies at large (Van Bueren 1998). Children are now often portrayed both in legal and in social science discourse as having a potential for self-actualization or self-realization (Eekelaar 1994, 49; Rogers 1989). Such a potential may be seen as enshrined within the concept of human dignity and justifying the attribution of human rights (Taylor 1994, 41–42; Eberle 2002, 256).

However, current legal protection of the child's right to human dignity does not guarantee protection of an individualized identity.

Taylor (1991, 32–35) explains that the notion of individualized identity draws support from an ideal of authenticity, in the sense of being true to oneself and to one's particular way of being. It implies that if you are not true to yourself; you miss what being human means for you.

The understanding of identity proposed here departs from the classical substantive, essentialist, conception of identity, which emphasizes static, unchanging elements of identity (Taylor 1991 and 1994; Lavie and Swedenberg 1996, 11; Krumer-Nevo and Malka 2012).

Fuller beautifully captures and exemplifies a facet of the dynamic conception of identity proposed here. We see how it departs from commonplace perceptions:

> Growing up, my friends and I expected to be the same person for life... But by the time I was fifty I could look back and identify several distinct personas that had taken up residence within and use me as a mouthpiece to make one or another case in the world. So could most of my friends. Initially we were embarrassed by this state of affairs, feeing it to be a sign of inconsistency and failure. Now I see it as metamorphosing from one identity to the next as a natural extension of the development from childhood to adolescence to early adulthood and beyond. The more flexible, forgiving attitude that results from a malleable self-model turns out to be the perspective we need to maintain our dignity in adversity and accord it to others in theirs. If we can't treat our current self with respect, what chance have we of doing so with anyone else?
>
> FULLER 2006, 132–133. See also KRUMER-NEVO and MALKA 2012

This vignette invites us to consider the tie between identity and human dignity as it is experienced.

Identity should not be seen as developing in vacuum, but rather always through dialogue and sometimes struggles with significant others- those persons who matter to the individual constructing his identity (Taylor 1994; Wilson 1997, 281; Eekelaar 1994, 51; Eekelaar 2004). Even as the individual outgrows some of these others, the internal dialogue with them continues throughout life and a contribution to the formation of an evolving identity in early childhood continues indefinitely (Taylor 1994). Taylor (1994) writes of two spheres of recognition of identity. First, the intimate sphere of recognizing an identity that is formed in dialogue and struggle with significant others, and second, a public sphere where a politics of recognition may protect the individual's identity. In adopting such a conception of identity, it is not difficult to accept the assertion of Lavie, Swedenberg and their colleagues that there is no objective immutable link between identity and a specific place such as, say, a place of birth (Lavie and Swedenburg 1996, esp. 1, 2).

An assumption of such a link is inherent in an abstract, decontextualized, understanding of identity rejected here.

Alongside the child's need 'to become', to develop and change, to fulfill dreams and plans, the need, in An-Na'im's words, 'to be different from others' (2002, 1–2) there is another need. This is often neglected by advocates of children's rights, though it is well embedded in social science literature. This is the child's need 'to be', to be his authentic self and to be recognized as 'somebody' when simply being that self (Feuerstein 1984; Feuerstein and Hoffman 1982, 44–45, 1982, 44–45; Bilsky 1997, 148–149; Engel and Munger 1996, esp. 48). This ensures the child's psychological survival.

A children's rights regime should ideally be responsive to the complementing needs 'to be' and 'to become'. We often perceive granting of a right to autonomy- responding to the child's need 'to become' and overcoming adult paternalism- as the most advanced and problematic stage in evolving child law (e.g. Franklin 1986, 27–38; Van Bueren 1998). When we do not empower children to develop unique personal identities they may see themselves simply in terms of their biological needs. Such children may become indifferent to their human rights or misuse them in a reductionist way to satisfy only momentary desires and impulses (Feuerstein and Hoffman 1982; 44–45) totally divorced from their noble purposes as envisioned and described in human rights theory and in case law (e.g. Cohn 1991, 19–21; Eekelaar 1994, 51).

Through an evolutionary process of choice between different identifications and values, the child constantly creates and recreates a personal identity until, we may hope, it crystallizes in adulthood (Zafran 2010; Van Praagh 1999b,

1348; Van Praagh 1997, 366; Wilson 1997, 282–282). We find classical portrayals of such processes of changing identifications in the lives of Nelson Mandela and Mahatma Gandhi (Mandela 2002; Erikson 1970; Gandhi 1994). Both individuals reached the stage of courageous commitment to a cultural identity despised and belittled by mainstream society only through lengthy processes of personal growth in their alliances and identifications. Both rejected sectarian conceptions of their identity often imposed or suggested by social and legal norms. Both allowed themselves to be themselves despite pressures to conform and to adopt a conventional identity.

2 *Does Legal Recognition of an Individualized Identity Imply Endorsement of a Traditional Liberal Individualist Ethos?*

A politics of equal dignity leads to recognizing the individual's eligibility to a uniform set of rights and immunities. This chapter proposes that we need a politics of difference or identity, which would call for recognizing a human being's unique individualized identity, and, which sees suppressing distinctness by a dominant or majority identity as the cardinal sin against authenticity, to use Taylor's (1994, 38) words. In her seminal chapter, Carol Gilligan (1982) can be understood as developing this charge in relation to silencing a distinct, caring voice, which has been derogatorily constructed as a feminine voice by mainstream academic and popular discourse. I argue, using Taylor's wording again, that Gilligan can be understood as showing how mainstream discourse presenting an atomistic image of the ideal human being, sins against both boys and girls. Such a model of humanness, often underlying public and legal discourse, denies or ignores a central psychological insight: human beings are naturally interdependent rather than independent (Hartling 2008; Gilligan 1982, 2, 4, 74; Freeman 1997, 73; Cohn 1991, 19, 21). This insight has been utilized to articulate a theory of children's rights, departing from a traditional ethos of liberal individualism in which the centrality of the child's right to the protection of his relationships with significant others is emphasized (e.g. Minow 1991, 267–311; Zafran 2010). An ethos of interdependence can serve as a basis for such a theory of rights. Universal protection of relationships with those others is, in fact, protection of the distinctness and the uniqueness in the individual. In this context, the universal and the particular converge.

Protecting the child's definition of identity, that is, protecting a child-constructed identity, may be construed as a derivative of a commitment to dignity (Taylor 1994; Raz 1998, 200) although dignity politics has not yet been utilized for this purpose: As Taylor (1994, 39) explains that this is an instance of a shift 'where a new understanding of the human social condition imparts a radically new meaning to an old principle'. To conclude, legal recognition of an individualized identity does not imply endorsement of a traditional liberal individualist ethos, as one might initially assume. It is founded on an alternative ethos of interdependence.

3 *Is Public Recognition of the Child's Individualized Identity Necessary in the Children's Rights Era?*

Society often tends to see the child as property of the state or parents to be molded in an other's image (Slaughter 2000). Our recognition of the child as an individual, whose authentic identity is worthy of respect, is meant to reaffirm our commitment to the child's unique humanness and counteracts such a tendency. One may doubt whether such commitment needs reaffirmation in an era in which – from the perspective of international law – children are seen as eligible for human rights. However, it is suggested here that law is only gradually moving away from serving those in positions of political and economic power as opposed to others, such as children and ethnic minorities, to safeguarding universally humane treatment and human rights for all (Lindner 2012, esp. 105–119; Nandy 1990, 32–33; Minow 1991, 7–10, 297). Historically, one can observe sad human inclination to allow exclusion, stigmatization and even victimization of the Other and then to deny, rationalize, repress or disassociate the painful experiences of the Other (Nandy 1990, 32–33; Minow 1991, 4, 5–7; Minow 1990b, 1673–1674, 1684). Society continues to withhold eligibility for rights and protection for self-actualization from those it sees as deviant, morally impaired or simply less than fully human. Communities, families and adults meaningful to the child may be seen in this way and therefore, the child's ties to them are liable to be disregarded. Furthermore, though children are seen by international law as bearers of rights, in practice, they are vulnerable and their participation in determining their futures through rights discourse is typically partial and unrelated to their actual competencies (Minow 1990a, 285, 303–304). Tendencies to see the child as not fully human and as property of the state or parents to be molded in another's image may be subtle, implicit, and even preconscious. Oppression, stigmatization, and social exclusion are seldom purposeful acts (Minow 1991, 62–65). Thus, children affiliated to minorities are in special jeopardy of social exclusion and silencing.

Admittedly, our moral commitment towards the child has grown since the Second World War through the assimilation of human rights norms into mainstream democratic culture (Van Bueren 1998a, 1–25; Alston 1994). This has also served to improve the general level of toleration to difference guaranteed by law. However, toleration as understood in liberal theory does not necessarily entail a commitment to viewing different cultures, which children sense as their own, as fundamentally equal in worth to mainstream culture: Not all that is tolerable is seen as of equal worth to ours. A commitment to multiculturalism encourages us to see children as of equal worth despite their different cultural identities and because of their common humanity (Raz 1998, 204–205). It calls for strengthening our capacity to identify and combat biases against the Other embedded in our upbringing and in professional training (Kinsella 2010; Minow 1990b) and to disclose publicly and overcome them. I contend here, that one such potential bias is the bias against culture as a context of personal meaning to the child.

Jonathan Sacks (1995, 118–119) too emphasizes that individuals are not abstractions. Liberal individualism wrongs the individual in as much as it allows societies to demand of the individual to abandon his group identity in order to be a rights bearing citizen. No one is justified in taking action to assimilate a minority group at the cost of threatening an individual's cultural identity. You cannot respect an individual solely through respecting his individuality. Respecting his sense of belonging is essential to respecting who he is.

A traditional ethos of liberal individualism commits us to avoid silencing minority opinion because it may be detrimental to the public good. Here, we go beyond such reasoning towards a deeper commitment to the child's human dignity. When we protect a child's ties with both his social family and his community, in as much as he relates to them with a sense of belonging, we may have to compromise protecting conformity to values that mainstream or minority communities see as worthy. This may be because the families of such children may not conform to socially accepted values or the child may not conform to family values. Failing to respect difference in this arena may be seen as effectively treating children as objects and as inconsistent with regarding them as rights holders (Featherstone, White and Morris 2014). For example, a child's family may promote middle-class values in a socialist or Marxist society; it may promote pacifism or universalism in a patriotic or militaristic society. Similarly, it may advocate moral superiority of religious law or community law over state law. Alternatively, a child may reject the values of his nuclear family of origin and reach out to the values of the extended family or community of origin. Liberal individualism does not offer the child the protection he needs in these cases.

Evelin Lindner (2012, 142, 2009, 154) explains that social identity complexity is gaining legitimacy. In the past, it was unwelcome: Power elites shaped social identity making it monolithic and denying individual free choice. Protecting the child's right to identity as a right to belonging, fostering a sense of belonging, threatens a social structure comprised of monolithic identities. Not surprisingly, power elites fear complex social identities. They do not make for obedient foot soldiers. Our identity structures become more inclusive and our toleration of out-groups increases when we recognize and accept such complexity.

I suggest that, if our aim is to ensure individual children are not, in effect, silenced, we must positively protect elements contributing to the molding of an authentic self. It is not enough for law to ensure that a child can express preferences freely, and that they are taken into account as article 12 mandates (Eekelaar 1994, 60, note 10). Law must positively ensure that the child's wishes and feelings are sought. Only if the law encourages the child's participation in defining who he is, can the child develop into an adult capable of expressing himself authentically. A commitment by the state to an ideal of authenticity would introduce a structured element of caution into state intervention in the field of child law. The benefits of such intervention can be more lucidly balanced with its drawbacks made apparent through recognition of an individualized identity.

I argue here that child law should challenge both mainstream and minority cultures to transform themselves by shouldering a commitment to the ideal of authenticity in relation to child rearing.

I do not envision an abrupt, violent process of transformation, but rather an evolutionary one. Thus, for example, the connotation of belonging may gradually change: As stated earlier, children are often perceived as belonging to their parents. Nevertheless, I do not suggest, we abandon the term 'belonging'. Rather, one can hope for the transformation of both the legal and common usage of the word belonging. Law's focus on protecting the child's sense of belonging may gradually change social norms towards a greater commitment to developing an authentic self.

Evelin Lindner (2009, 151) explains that when we do not satisfy the universal need for belonging, we compromise human dignity. People thirsting for belonging are sometimes willing to put status higher than health and survival. They voluntarily humiliate their own humanity.

The consequences for society's democratic fabric can be most harmful. Adults with an unmet belonging need are vulnerable to being evilly and slyly turned into handicapped and thus harmless inferiors in the ranked systems abundant in our societies. If people believe that they can increase their sense of belonging by climbing up the ladder in a ranked system, even at the cost of mutilating themselves or others, silencing authentic thought and speech, they may fall for this trap and do so. Lindner calls this process voluntary self-humiliation to highlight that we can unmask and undo it; she agrees it would be more correct to say that people are unwittingly manipulated into self-humiliation. Through this dynamic, Lindner highlights how responding to the need for belonging is essential for dignifying humanity and humans.

To summarize: I argue here, that despite wide legal recognition of the child's eligibility to human rights, the legal recognition of an individualized identity is necessary to reaffirm society's commitment to the child as a human being in its own right.

4 *How Can Law Protect not only the Child's Right 'to Become' but also His Right 'to Be'?*

I have introduced the child's needs 'to be' and 'to become'. The question remains how we can practically protect both.

Self-definition can never take place in a vacuum: A child knows who he is only within a specific familial and community context (Wilson 1997, 281), however dull at times. Besides being cared for, a child needs a familial and communal environment, which he feels is his and which affords him a clear understanding of who he is and helps to give meaning to his life (Hassall 1994). The child's family and community are his starting points in life. Ideally, these are his family of origin and community of origin. From within a family and a community child naturally begins to create meaningful ties and develop an identity that evolves over time. His experiences are gradually applied to new and widening fields beyond his family and community of origin as he matures biologically and emotionally.

The legal definition of family, however well-informed by social science literature, is ultimately a cultural construction. Nevertheless, legal rhetoric sometimes inaccurately gives us the impression that such a definition captures some eternal truths (Minow 1987, 959–960). Thus, neither 'blood ties' nor 'legal ties' of parenthood necessarily stand for psychological ties with a child. In order to discover who fills the role of mother or father for the child, it is essential that recourse be made to the child's subjective perceptions. In practical terms, protecting the child's right 'to be' primarily means ensuring that he will not be forced to disown his authentic familial and communal identity, to the detriment of his sense of self and of his human dignity in order to gain recognition of his normalcy by mainstream society (Bilsky 1997, 144–145; Hassall 1994, 2–3).

'Closed' adoption cases exemplify the need for such protection. 'Closed' adoption- breaking all ties with biological kin- was regarded in the not too distant past as the ideal way to guarantee secure and uninterrupted parenting and family life. Nowadays, the child's loss of earlier relationships along with all traces of their pre-adoption identity is widely recognized as potentially damaging to some children and a movement to greater openness in adoption is drawing growing support (Siegel 2013; Ryan et al. 2011).

A helpful illustration of the unmet need 'to be' has come from research into the long-term experiences of adopted adults (Feast and Howe 2000).

Research shows that having a name or maintaining stable ties with one's psychological parents, guaranteed under the Convention, is not enough. Adopted adults who were not seeking substitute psychological parents still wanted to meet their birth parents (Feast and Howe 2000). Many reported that they satisfied in this way important concerns about their personal identity and filled a void that they felt (Feast and Howe 2000, 387). I suggest that such searches express the adults' unmet need 'to be' in childhood and adolescence.

Feeling protected in being who he is, a child can then allow himself to 'recreate' himself in fantasy and in real life: to dream his own dreams, wish his own wishes and even implement his own plans, however small scale they may be, at first. Through interdependent relationships with his environment, he grows to be increasingly autonomous yet, as explained above, never fully independent (Gilligan 1982, 74; Minow 1991, 301–303; Freeman 1997, 73; Hartling 2008).

The strength and significance of children's ties to a family and community they define as theirs can vary. Some children are alienated from both their extended and nuclear families. These children often develop unique relationships, which may seem peculiar to the untrained eye. These may be ties to carers, teachers or therapists. These ties give us the opportunity to question the validity of rigid Conventional boundaries defining who is considered as family and what is considered professional behavior. They prod us to challenge the abovementioned assumption that the legal definition of family captures some eternal truths. It is only possible to understand these relationships in light of the problematics of the children's upbringing and development. Atypical responses to abnormal circumstances are often the wisest and most creative. Thus, the law should respond cautiously to these relationships and avoid attempts to dictate rigidly that only preconceived relationships serve the child's best interests.

The definition of the right to identity should enable the decision-maker to understand that the little the child sees as his identity, should, in principle, be protected. This understanding of the child's circumstances will enable the decision to ensure that not only does the child maintain existing ties, but also that he can develop new ones arising from his world. The experience gained through approximately a century of state intervention in the name of the Best Interests Principle teaches a lesson of caution. Fantasies of saving children may turn out to be painful for the children involved if we do not hear and understand them as human beings possessing a unique identity. Ties to imperfect blameworthy carers were too often neglected (Hassall 1994, 9–10; Van Praagh 1999a, 156; Van Praagh 1999b, 1348; Kufeldt 1993, 9–10). Imposing well-intentioned adult minded plans brought about the result that children sometimes grow up to become alienated adults unable to relate trustingly and caringly (Kufeldt 1993).

If professionals – including legal professionals – listen attentively to children and understand what children consider meaningful in their personal world, children may succeed in challenging their exclusion. They may thus grow up to trust future representatives of normative society and to identify with its norms (Minow 1991, 297–299). Respecting the child's sense of belonging may promote identification with society (Raz 1998, 203–204).

The overall outcome of this approach would be greater legal protection to the child's ties to his family and community of origin. Nevertheless,, in certain cases, law may protect significant ties a child has developed to a family and community which he was not born into, thus overriding the interests of biological parents and minority communities.

A classic example of such cases would be a case in which foster parents who took into their home a neglected child through child protection proceedings are allowed to adopt a child despite rehabilitation of his biological parents. These biological parents may have had a history of drug abuse, criminality and homelessness. Their rehabilitation in such a case is undoubtedly morally admirable. Nevertheless, the parents' objections to the adoption may be outweighed by a child's clear-cut wishes and feelings if the child is accorded a right to an individualized identity, and law becomes responsive to his sense of belonging.

The new meaning of the right to identity I propose here offers the child state intervention that is not systematically available at present. It seeks to ensure that, by protecting ties that he holds valuable, the child sees himself as neither the property of his parents nor of any other person or organ, such as a state welfare agency.

However, the legal system lacks the tools to safeguard fully the child's sense of belonging in every single case. Law cannot accommodate all human sensitivities and is inevitably based on no more than an approximation of what the child experiences (Eekelaar 1994, 46–47).

This notwithstanding, the proposed definition of a child's right to identity offers reinforcement for the safeguards protecting the child's human dignity. It rejects the notion of a 'normal' identity, which it does not replace it with the endorsement of ethnocentrism, connoting the position that only black or white or brown is beautiful, a position regrettably associated with identity politics (Minow 1996). Rejecting ethnocentrism while respecting the relevance of ethnicity in the construction and reconstruction of an individualized identity may lessen the exploitation of identity politics to promote community interests at the individual's expense (Deng 2002, 188–189; Alston and Gilmour-Walsh 1996, 39). Indeed, for every 'we' there is 'them'. We are habituated to boundaries between friends and strangers and these and other boundaries it is questionable whether we would have an identity (Sacks 2002, 46). However, the boundaries do not have to be static. We may, as individuals and as a society, see these boundaries as an invitation to expand continually our awareness of inequity to the Other and to overcome a sense of threat when facing difference. Identity and a sense of belonging do not have to exclude any specific unchangeable Other from eligibility to rights (Nandy 1990, 32; Sacks 2002, 46–66). If we see otherness as an invitation to care for the Other and thus respect his human rights, for example, through the universally recognized Golden Rule (An-Na'im 1994, 68; Cohn 1991, 42), we become less alienated from him (Erikson 1963). Identity – 'mine' and 'his', 'ours' and the 'theirs' – can be dynamic and can become more inclusive. Ethnic distinctions may thus lose their significance as rigid personal boundaries that define identity (Eekelaar 2004).

The child's right to identity, informed by an understanding of authenticity, offers to exchange the imagery of universal uniformity with an imagery of difference and uniqueness in the way children relate to their personal worlds (Minow 1996; Van Praagh 1999a, 203). A right to a cultural identity, relying on the child's definition of who he is, assumes the dialectic of change described above (Van Praagh 1999b, 1348; Van Praagh 1997, 366; Cooper, Baistow, Hetherington, Pitts and Spriggs 1995, 136–139). What the child defines presently as his identity may change in the future, as his identity continues to evolve. The state's commitment to upholding the child's human dignity, a commitment to his identity as a person developing towards autonomous adulthood, should 'accompany' the child in his journey. A possible derivative of the evolution in the child's identity is a change in commitment to different cultures, including minority cultures.

To conclude, under ideal conditions, a child's nuclear and extended family, his culture, language and nationality are his 'birth right' (Hassall 1994), which he enjoys without any intervention from the law. Thus, his need 'to be' more than his need 'to become' is naturally protected. Family law should aspire to draw children's life closer to the ideal, while recognizing its inherent incapacity, ever fully to achieve this aim. Having said that, the legal protection of the right to identity as outlined here, does have the capacity to safeguard a critical factor relating to the child's well-being, namely personal ties that are significant to him.

5 *Culture as a Context of Personal Meaning; Beyond Cultural Sensitivity*

Which culture should a child be allowed to enjoy (for example, example according to Article 30 of the Convention)? Which is his culture, say in the case of a child with multiple minority affiliations, biological parents from one minority, foster parents with which he lived from age two to six or adoptive parents? Is it the biological family's minority culture, that is, the culture into which the child was born, or is it the minority culture of the foster family, which raised him from ages two to eight? Perhaps, it is the minority culture of the adoptive family from which he is separated when he leaves for boarding school? Perhaps the peer culture at the boarding school?

The conception suggested here is that from a child-centered perspective, the culture that the child should be allowed to enjoy, whether mainstream or minority, is not an abstract derivative of the decision maker's theoretical knowledge. From the perspective of the individual child, it is irrelevant how the tenets and lifestyle of Orthodox Judaism or Shiite Islam are described in any textbook. The child's lived experience may be different from those descriptions. The child's culture as uniquely experienced by the individual child is defined here as a set of related meanings by which the child interprets the reality of his life and its unique circumstances (Kline 1992). This uniqueness is a universal human condition: By acknowledging that as he grows, each child develops a unique cultural identity brings into focus the commonality of children's experience of identity formation rather than the 'otherness' of the child's unique excluded culture or experience (Minow 1999a, 24).

Although it is important to understand the different stages of childhood development and children's psychological needs derivative of them, such understanding is, in itself, not enough to enable society to respond to children's needs: It may even serve to disempower the child (Eekelaar 1994). Such understanding reflects only an approximation of the child's experience. Already from the first months of their lives, children have both the capacity and interest in giving meaning to events, although admittedly, they are often immature decision-makers. We are therefore called upon to explore the relationship between the meaning the child gives to events throughout his life which influence his preferences and the legal decisions pertaining to those preferences. It is not suggested that the right to identity should guarantee the child a power of veto in decisions pertaining to him. However, ignoring the meanings the child gives to his world by imposing different meanings regarding what is good and valuable for the child, and by not offering protection for culture as a construct of the child, can be detrimental to the child's quality of life. Not only can this reduce the efficacy of our efforts on the child's behalf, but it can also cause him to experience life generally as duller and society as alienating (see also Eekelaar 1994, 54).

Commitment to cultural sensitivity did not secure the child the protection I am advocating for. Furthermore, through conceptualizing culture as unchanging and timeless, children were incarcerated in 'their' cultures in the name of cultural sensitivity (Lavie and Swedenburg 1996, 3; Koptiuch 1996, 215–233). I call for an empathic and respectful understanding of the individual child's experience. Achieving such an understanding within a legal setting is a worthy challenge for professionals.

III International Law

1 *Specific References to Identity in the United Nations Convention on the Rights of the Child*

In Articles 7, 8 and 9, the Convention guarantees the child's rights to a name, to citizenship, to know his parents and not to be separated from them respectively. Article 8 leaves the impression that identity is an open-ended concept. The attributes of identity, namely, nationality, name and family relations, are mentioned illustratively implied by the word 'including' (Hodgson 1993, 265). The The next article in which we find explicit referral to the child's identity is Article 29. This chapter states the aims of children's education, that is, that it should encourage the child to respect his own cultural identity and that of others from different cultures. Article 30 guarantees the right of the minority and indigenous child 'to enjoy his or her own culture'. Nothing in the Convention defines culture or what makes one a minority or indigenous child. No article in the Convention or the different sets of guidelines deriving from the Convention explicitly guarantees the child a right to preserve what he sees as his cultural identity or to preserve ties that are meaningful to him, to respect his individualized identity or to ensure specifically his involvement in defining his identity.

Questions such as these arise: Do only minority children need law's protection? What of undemocratic regimes in which most of the political and economic power is in the hands of an elite belonging to an ethnic minority?

There is no explicit answer to such questions in the text of the Convention.

2 *The European Convention on Human Rights and Fundamental Freedoms*

The European Convention contributes little to the definition of identity, beyond adopting a proactive approach to the duty of the state to protect family life (Bainham 2000, 483–484). It does not explicitly mention the child's right to identity. There is an implied reference to safeguarding the child's right to identity in Article 8, which positively obliges ratifying states to uphold the individual's right to respect for family life. However, as Bainham (2000, 483–484) maintains, it is unclear what the child's right to family life implies. The European Court of Human Rights ruled that the interest of knowing one's origins is protected by article 8 (Frowein 2002, 130–131). However, much remains unclear. If knowledge of one's origins destabilizes the child's family life, which of the child's interests takes precedence and must be protected? How is the interest to be balanced against other interests protected by rights such as the right to state intervention on his behalf or the right to parental guidance both of which may safeguard the child's emotional well-being? To what extent will the interest of knowing one's parents be protected? No answer is given in either the wording of the European Convention or in the interpretation of the Convention offered by the Jurisprudence of the European Court. To conclude, explicit referrals to identity in these key international legal documents do not provide a legal framework which may protect a child-constructed identity.

The next section examines the relationship between Articles 5, 12 and 13 of the Convention. I suggest how the implicit references to identity-related rights that they contain can help us to develop a conceptual framework beyond the explicit references to identity in the Convention.

3 *The United Nations Convention on the Rights of the Child: The Overall Picture*

As noted earlier, the provisions of the Convention relating specifically to the child's identity do not explicitly protect the child's individualized identity. One cannot, however, understand the Convention's position fully by relating solely to these provisions.

I suggest that the Convention as a whole shows that conceptually, it supports the meaning of the right to identity proposed here.

The preamble states:

> [...] the parties to the Convention are] convinced that the family, as the fundamental group of society and the natural environment for the growth and well-being of all its members and particularly children, should be afforded the necessary protection and assistance so that it can fully assume its responsibilities within the community.

Article 18. 2, for its part, enjoins the state to protect and support family life:

> For the purpose of guaranteeing and promoting the rights set forth in the present Convention, State parties shall render appropriate assistance to parents and legal guardians in the performance of their child-rearing responsibilities and shall ensure the development of institutions, facilities and for the care of children.

Article 20, like the preamble, can be seen as seeking to protect the child's ties to a personal world. However, there is no mention of identity in the article:

> When considering solutions [for children temporarily or permanently deprived of their family environment, or in whose best interests cannot be allowed to remain in that environment] due regard shall be paid to the desirability of continuity in a child's upbringing and to the child's ethnic, religious, cultural and linguistic background.

Article 5 of the C, while also not mentioning the word identity, offers an important key to understanding the Convention's intended protection of the child's identity. It reads as follows:

> State parties shall respect the responsibilities, and duties of parents or, where applicable, the members of the extended family or community as provided for by local custom, legal guardians or other persons legally responsible for the child, to provide, in a manner consistent with the evolving capacities of the child, appropriate direction and guidance in the exercise by the child of the rights recognized in the present Convention.

This article clearly frames a broad general principle, and also has a key role to play in interpreting the provisions of the Convention. It creates a new basis for the relationship between the child, the family and state. This basis supports the rationale for defining the right to identity as I propose here. Namely: the state's primary responsibility towards the child is to respect the role of the nuclear and extended family and of the community in the child's life, rather than to intervene in order to protect the child from them.

A tension exists between article 5 and articles 12 and 13, which grant the child a right to be heard, a right to participate in decisions relating to him and a right to free expression – rights that can override parents' wishes. It is not difficult to contemplate situations in which parents entrusted to guide the child in exercising rights would be tempted to obstruct the child from doing so, because of their own selfish interests (Fortin 1998, 42; Freeman 1997, 68). However, I suggest, that Article 5, through its moderation, generality and relative ambiguity, can, when understood in combination with Articles 12 and 13, contribute to an evolutionary process, which will advance the child's legal status. The Convention thus encourages adults with whom the child maintains meaningful ties to find culturally appropriate ways to respect the rights of the child, including his right to participation in decisions relating to him.

Delegates from the Southern hemisphere who took part in the drafting, adoption and implementation of human rights norms did not operate with concepts and mechanisms from their own political, cultural and ideological history. Thus, the universal human rights consensus reached is elusive (An-Na'im 1994, 65).

By trusting families and communities to respect children's rights and by not derogating from their cultures and traditions, the Convention (primarily through article 5) offers families and communities a respectful challenge. Thus, although, the terminology of human rights originated in Europe and was mainly developed by the West, we cannot easily dismiss the Convention's invitation to respect children's rights as patronizing, alien, imperialistic or Eurocentric.

We should welcome the tension between Articles 5, 12 and 13, and the legal complexity it produces since it reflects the real-life complexity of responding to the child's conflicting needs 'to be' and 'to become'.

Essentially, through this tension the Convention overcomes the temptation to entertain a crude atomistic vision of the child's interests. Our discussion illustrates that by endeavoring to reach a balance between protection rights and participation rights, the Convention is not a children's liberation manifesto: Clearly, it does not purport to free children subjugated by adults. I suggest that it does not abandoning children to some of their rights. Children who exercise participation rights and civil rights and also enjoy protected adult guidance have a greater chance to develop into more rounded adults, adults who can, not only exercise autonomy, but also function within relationships of commitment and responsibility (Freeman 1997, 37–40; Smith 1997, 103).

This scenario, in which the child's evolving capacities are recognized within the guidance and protection of adults may be threatened because of the inadequate protection offered to the child's right to identity. Adults are often tempted to dismiss what a child says. For example, they may describe his input as immature and an expression of ignorance, 'programming' or 'brainwashing' (Ronen 1998). Thus, for example, through diagnosis of the controversial Parental Alienation Syndrome, some courts have been persuaded to order a child who is functioning well both emotionally and intellectually to live with a parent whom he hates or in a state institution. This may happen even if the hated parent was abusive toward the child and there are objective reasons for the child's aversion to him, as long as brainwashing against the hated parent by the other parent is proven (Bruch 2001; Bala 1999, 194–195). Thus, there is a real risk that Article 12 will be emptied of meaning through paternalistic notions of protecting children from influence and coercion. (Ronen 1998, 257–259; Eekelaar 1994, 56–57).

If a child has legal recourse to a claim for consideration of his wishes or feelings because these wishes or feelings indicate ties that are meaningful to him, his participation in decisions relating to him may become more visible and influential. In such circumstances, recognizing a child's right to be heard and to participate in decisions concerning him and to express himself freely, may enhance the weight given to the child's definition of family, community and culture and may allow implementing article 12 in a manner that overcomes the prima fascia tension with article 5. Once we recognize a child-constructed right to identity, the tension between Articles 5, 12, 13 may serve the healthy development of the child's identity.

IV Identity is Two Cases

1 *The Judges' Narratives*

We shall now examine two English Court of Appeal cases introduced at the outset of this chapter attempting to implement the proposed redefinition of the right to identity:

Re M (Section 94 Appeals)

This case concerned a seven-year-old girl, whom the court called S. The girl's parentage was of mixed race, her mother being white and her father black. The parents were never married and upon the breakdown of their relationship, the father had unsupervised contact with the child, which was stopped by the mother from time to time. Proceedings before the Family Proceeding Courts ended in the magistrates granting the mother's application to end the contact between the child and the father. The father appealed under Section 94 of the Children Act 1989 and Ewbank J. dismissed the appeal. The father then appealed against the decision to the Court of Appeal. The decision in the Appeal was written by Butler-Loss LJ, Kennedy LJ concurring.

Butler-Sloss LJ explained that the appeal was remitted for rehearing because the judge did not advert at all in his judgment to the 'major' issue of race and to the failure of the magistrates to deal with it. The Judge linked the failure to deal with the question of race to other factors:

> The mother and her new husband are white and the father is black. The child whose photograph I have seen is clearly of mixed race. The court welfare officer was troubled by the ending of the contact when she felt the child would wonder why she did not see her father, especially since she is a mixed-race child. She had said she was getting a new white daddy.

> The court welfare officer felt the child was confused about her racial identity, and on my reading of the reports and the oral evidence, there was at least a hint of the mother and grandmother shutting their eyes to this important issue. The welfare officer asked for an adjournment for 6 months to enable contact at a contact center to continue and be monitored. The magistrates made findings adverse to the father that he showed little interest in the child's schooling had little insight into the child's emotional or developmental needs and did not meet financial obligations. Although some of these findings were against the views of the court welfare officer, magistrates were entitled to make their own findings .... The child had said she did not want to see her father but the court welfare officer did not believe that such was the child's underlying view and gave reasons. The magistrates ought in my view at least to have indicated their disagreement with the court welfare officer on the issues of child's behavior and her wishes, which they clearly thought significant. The magistrates decided that the contact had not added anything positive to S's upbringing and the father had not shown sufficient commitment and dedication to deal with the complex situation, in particular the degree of hostility by the mother and grandmother towards him.

The reasoning of the decision given by Butler-Sloss LJ offers some substantive guidance to the judge re-hearing the case:

> Whether in the future this father will have any contact at all, frequent contact, infrequent contact or indirect contact, will be a matter for the judge rehearing the application. He will have to consider the significance of race and the hostility of the maternal family towards the father and place those and all the other factors for and against the father having contact to the child in the balance in coming to the decision on contact. But the child's racial origins and the concerns of the court welfare officer have to be carefully considered and it is for those reasons that I felt this appeal has to be allowed.

Below, I shall critically examine this reasoning leading to an outcome I consider wrong from a child centered perspective.

Re M (Child's Upbringing)

In this case, the care and adoption of a 10-year-old black African boy of Zulu parentage was contested between his biological parents and a white foster mother. The boy, called P by the court, was born in South Africa to a mother who worked as a nanny and cook/housekeeper in the house of the foster mother who had three daughters. The mother was not married to the father who also worked for the foster mother for a while. From the age of eighteen months, the boy lived with the foster mother in her home in a way that would enable him to remain there with his mother instead of being sent back to his mother's village according to Apartheid regulations. The boy and the white employer became closely attached to each other. The father had only sporadic contacts with the child and his mother. It appears that at some stage during P's early years, the father had a relationship with another woman who bore him a child. In 1992, when the child was six, the foster mother decided to leave South Africa for London because she regarded the political situation as unstable and was worried about possible violence. When the foster mother decided to leave, P's parents agreed that he move with her. It is noteworthy that, according to Thorpe J, who heard the case at first instance, 'the appellant's first preference would have been to take both the mother and P with her to London, but the mother made it plain that she would not leave her homeland. The easiest course in practical terms would have been to have left [P] behind with [the mother]. But she had by then a strong attachment to the child. Those attachments led her to offer to continue to take care of [P] and to provide for him, as though he were her own child. The only issue between the parties is as to the duration of the arrangement. [the appellant] asserts that it was an indefinite arrangement that would endure until the completion of [P's] education. [The father and the mother] assert that the arrangement was for five years precisely. It seems to me that reality lies somewhere between those poles. On arrival in the UK in March 1992, the foster mother told the immigration authorities that she wished to adopt P and P was given leave to remain in the UK for three months. By May 1992, the foster mother had already reached a firm decision, unknown to the parents that she wished to adopt P. In October 1992 she wrote to the mother the following:

> To keep [P] in this country, I have to adopt him. If there is another way to do it, I will. I will never take him away from you, so that you won't be able to see him again. You are his mother.

Soon after that, the parents were visited by a social worker at the foster mother's request in order to establish their wishes as to P's adoption. The parents initially objected to the adoption and the mother spoke of not hearing from the child since July. A few days later the social worker wrote again to say that the mother's position appeared to have changed. She was proposing that if P stayed in England, he should visit his biological parents each year for a month. Later, both parents expressed the position that if the foster mother wanted to take the child forever – breaking the agreement with them – the child should return to them as soon as possible.

Between June and August 1993, the mother wrote ten letters, some of them dispatched within days of each other, in which the mother pleaded for the child's return to South Africa for a visit. In July 1993, the foster mother wrote a letter telling the mother that she could not send P to South Africa at that stage. The Judge described the letter as 'a surprisingly dispassionate response to what were moving appeals'.

He concluded that the father was an insubstantial figure in the child's life, as the only communication between him and the child was one Christmas card.

His appraisal of the relationship between the biological mother and the foster mother, quoted by the Court of Appeal, is particularly noteworthy:

> The correspondence shows the closeness of the relationship between [the mother] and [the appellant's] family. It further shows the tragic evaporation of trust and affection, gradual but steady. It is significant that the correspondence peters from frequent and intense to non-existent after the commencement of litigation.

In 1996, four years after the initial separation from his biological parents, the court gave its judgment. The court could have chosen between three options arising from the parties' positions: adoption (as sought by the foster mother), immediate return to South Africa (as sought by the parents) and a return to South Africa at the end of a period dictated by the court.

The court decided to adopt a fourth alternative. It laid down a master plan for the child's return to South Africa after a period of two years in which the child would be reintroduced to 'his' family and 'his' country, to use the court's words. In two years' time, the court would decide the dates and the circumstances of the child's permanent return to South Africa. The white foster mother was to pay for the travel expenses of the parents to England and of the child to South Africa. She could not afford most of her undertakings, as she became unemployed. She appealed against the order of the Judge on the basis that the review should reopen the issue of the child's residence and upbringing during adolescence. The child's biological parents appealed contending that the child's return should not be further delayed.

An expert psychiatrist appointed by the court explained the dangerous consequences of forcefully and prematurely removing the child from the foster mother and her family:

> To remove him in the middle of turmoil of disagreement would be very profoundly damaging, to such an extent that the boy might never recover his poise and psychological well-being and confidence.

Although it was clear from the expert opinion that the child's mind was set very strong against return, the court allowed the appeal of the parents. Ward LJ, quoting from another case, implied that allowing the child to remain in the UK would create a great danger of slipping into social engineering. The boy was returned to South Africa. The child 'was so unhappy in South Africa that he was later returned to England, into the care of the foster mother's (Fortin 1998, 357, note 10). In this case, too, I shall reexamine judicial reasoning leading to a result I question from a child-centered perspective.

2 *Counter-Narratives*

Re M (Section 94, Appeals)

Butler-Loss LJ writes that the magistrates thought the child's wishes were significant, and that they disagree with the court welfare officer as to the child's underlying views. However, we learn little about how the girl saw her father or how they related to each other. The Court of Appeal does not instruct the Judge rehearing the case to look into questions, which are fundamental to the child's psychological well-being: Does she love her father? Does she care about him at all? Does she feel sorry for him? Is she proud of him? Does she ever dream of living in her father's home or of her father looking after her?

Without answers to these or similar questions, which relate to the meaning of the parent- child tie, we know little of this facet of the child's individualized identity.

The judges disparage the father's parental functioning for apparently valid reasons. However, when deciding on parental contact, the child's sense of belonging and even psychological parenthood remain unmentioned.

Nothing in the UN Convention or the European Convention dictates a different outcome.

Nevertheless, the analysis I offer here suggests it is less significant the child says she has a 'white daddy' than she says she has a 'new daddy' (see also Eekelaar 2004). It is supported both by recognition of the child's need 'to be' underlying the child's right to identity and by psycholegal literature (Eekelaar 1994, 48). The court should have asked how a seven-year-old child who has known her father from birth can be reconciled with the fact that suddenly she has a 'new father'. The Court should have explicitly assumed that a non-racially mixed child, a child who is not confused about her racial identity, would also be inclined to 'wonder' why her father had disappeared.

The magistrates' choice of words is troubling: We learn that they ended contact mainly because the father had not added anything to the child's upbringing. However, a father is part of the child's being. A child may see her father as emotionally belonging to her even is he does nothing intentional for her and even if one cannot point to anything specific, which he added to her upbringing. As an interdependent human being, the child's needs her father and not a father even when he adds nothing visible to her upbringing.

Rosenblatt (1996), who is generally supportive of the Court of Appeal's decision, rightly points out that nurturing the 'ethnic child' toward sound psychological development could be more problematic than that of the white child as the latter does not have to face a society which rejects his 'ethnic' parent. I suggest we go beyond Rosenblatt's championing of the court's 'racial and ethnic awareness' (1996, 641). The court's reasoning reflects a color conscious yet vague and impersonal image of the child's identity. This image is unsatisfactory from a child-centered perspective.

If the father has no significance in his daughter's life, if she perceives him as not caring about her emotional needs, then being entitled to an individualized identity, she should not be forced to see him only because of a similarity in skin color. If this is her perception of him, and she is forced to see him, it is doubtful that such meeting would bolster her self-esteem concerning her racial identity. If, on the other hand, the child's father is significant to her, and she wishes to be in touch with him despite her mother's hostility towards him, it is not the similarity of their skin color that should be the deciding factor. In the latter case, the court must strike a difficult balance between the child's right to participation and self-constructed identity and her right to a stable psychologically nurturing family life.

The mother and grandmother are hostile to the father and may be shutting their eyes to the child's confusion about her racial identity. Their hostility may be only to the father as an individual, or it may amount to racial prejudice.

The court could have made this distinction and suggested that in both cases, the child's wishes and feelings may be harmfully influenced by their attitudes, and that they have a right and duty to guide the child in implementing her rights, being loyal to her interests in this task.

The court's judgment misses the opportunity to draw attention to the fine line between the sphere of imperfect yet legitimate adult guidance and influence and what lies beyond such a sphere and amounts to violation of the child's rights through programming. It also does not clarify, that we can deduce whether intervention is the least detrimental alternative from the individual child's perspective from the child's wishes and feelings.

To summarize: the Court of Appeal addresses the question of race in the abstract. Butler Sloss LJ does not direct our attention to the child's individualized identity, as perceived and constructed by the child and does not see the court as duty-bound to protect such an identity. Thus, the court's decision – I assume, unintentionally – serves ethnocentrism. The child's right to be in touch with the person she considers her father is overshadowed by efforts to ensure that the break of relationship with a black father will not adversely influence her feelings about being dark skinned. We can easily justify the court's instructions to the Judge rehearing the case, if we resorts to the common perception of cultural sensitivity or to the interests of the black community or black children at large. However, from the individual child's perspective, the pivotal question was not that of 'the child's racial origins' as such, but rather what the child sees as emotionally belonging to him. The court neglected this pivotal question. In practice, the difference between the two may be subtle at times, yet it is important to make the distinction.

Re M (Child's Upbringing)

Both Neill LJ and Ward LJ wrote detailed judgments. The closing passage written by Neill LJ is revealing. In it he explains why the child must be returned:

> Anyone who has studied this case cannot fail to have great admiration for the appellant and for the love and affection, which she and her family have given to P since he was a baby. But, he has the right to be reunited with his Zulu parents and with his extended family in South Africa.

The 'yes, but' dynamic of this pronouncement is similar to a passage in an American child abuse case, the DeShaney Case, discussed by Minow (Minow 1990b, 1674–1675). The passage starts with an empathic response, deriving from an almost instinctive sense of human interconnectedness, and ends with what seems to be an unavoidable rational decision, which must overcome the initial empathic response. I suggest, that because jurists are conditioned to dichotomize reason and emotion, to ignore our common interdependence and to delegitimize empathy as a decision-making tool, the legal conclusion, in opposition to the judges' empathic response, may seem even more unavoidable.

I suggest the conclusion is not unavoidable from a child-centered perspective.

I question Neill LJ's seemingly straightforward implementation of the child's 'right' to be reunited with 'his' family. I see his decision may be seen as an implicit unrecognized determination in a conflict of rights, between the right to be unified with one's biological nuclear and extended family and the right to remain with one's foster mother who is a psychological mother and with her family (Freeman 1997, 13–14, note 87). By denying paramountcy to the psychological parenthood, the court may be denying the child the opportunity to grow psychologically towards adulthood through dynamically defining and constructing an authentic identity. Consequently, the duty to give due weight to the child's wishes under Article 12 may be almost emptied of meaning.

Jane Fortin accurately identifies the 'undercurrent' of the court's rationale (with which she apparently agrees) when she writes (1998, 357):

> In Re M (Child's Upbringing), the Court of Appeal was effectively asked to redress the perpetration of racial injustice by a white South African woman who had produced a situation whereby P, a ten-year-old boy of Zulu parents, had stronger ties of affection for her and her family that he did for his own parents. The case was a complex one. In particular, there was the slightly unsavory background which suggested that the white foster mother had deceived P's birth parents over her true intentions when gaining their consent to her taking P with her when she came to England.

I see no reason to doubt that Neil LJ sincerely tried to be culturally sensitive. Furthermore, his decision is, strictly speaking, in accordance with both the UN Convention and the European Convention, as analyzed above. Nevertheless, one may well ask:

Does the official, dominant narrative of a white woman perpetrating racial injustice against her black former employee reflect the authentic experience of the individuals involved?

Was the resulting situation one-sidedly or mainly 'produced' by one individual?

Does the official storyteller, namely the Judge, go beyond trying to act in a way that is commonly perceived as culturally sensitive and seek to relate empathically to the individuals involved?

My answer to these questions is no.

By highlighting and reinterpreting certain facts, I would like to offer a counter-narrative, as lawyers often do in courtrooms (Ferguson 1996, 86). In this counter-narrative, I try to expose and counteract an unintentionally politicized selectivity of compassion. Let me (re)start by pointing out that the child was not raised in a Zulu environment after the age of eighteen months.

Since that age, the foster mother, with the biological mother's consent and approval, had brought the child up. This was in order to tackle an apartheid regulation mandating that the child return to his mother's village. The foster mother's family objected to her close ties with the blacks. She may have had to deceive both her family of origin, which was supportive of Apartheid regulations and apartheid authorities in order to maintain guardianship of the child. Deceit may have been a necessary ingredient for survival in the foster mother's world. If we find fault with the foster mother's deceitfulness, why not also consider her more politically-correct deceitfulness? Could it be that deceitfulness becomes a coping strategy too easily sought once used by necessity? It was also not contested the foster mother suggested the boy's biological mother accompany her to England, and the mother refused because she would not leave her homeland. There was no clear agreement as to the duration of the child's stay in England. Even after the foster mother asked for the biological parents' consent to adoption, at one stage the biological mother was prepared to agree that the child 'live' in England if he would visit her every year for a month. The most remarkable fact to be emphasized in such a counter-narrative would be the child's return to England with the consent of his biological parents after they gained full guardianship of him.

My efforts to understand empathically the individuals involved identify no villain, only imperfect human beings. These individuals are not always fully aware of their interdependence. They try to act decently and even lovingly in a difficult social reality, and sometimes fail.

The foster mother was not carrying out a master plan to break the ties between the child and the biological parents through her initially secret efforts to adopt the child. It was the mother's choice to remain in South Africa. However, at some stages, the foster mother's attachment to the child did not bring out the best in her. As noted by the court, her dispassionate response to the mother's painful letters indicates a blatantly insensitive attitude towards the child's biological mother. Nor did the parents have a master plan first to use the foster mother-a widow with three girls of her own- to raise their child, and then betray her trust by demanding her separation from him, when it suited their personal plans.

They initially enjoyed the love and generosity the foster mother offered the child, but her behavior maneuvered them into a position of opposition.

What is remarkable in this case is what was created and not what was later ruined: The case exemplifies how clear cut racist definitions of otherness are challenged and overcome through care and trust between two women attached to the same child. For a while, familial, communal and ethnic boundaries are ignored. Bitterness and distrust between the two women could have surfaced only after alienation was initially overcome.

Human frailties seem to explain better than any other reason the breakdown of relations primarily between the two women who initially cared both about each other and for the child and were struggling to do their best in challenging circumstances.

I suggest that, as in Solomon's dilemma, the court must identify the solution that holds most compassion for the child. King Solomon attempting to identify the psychological mother was aided by the fact that one of the women was ready to give up the child to save his life: Through her decision, she demonstrated her greater compassion for the child. My interpretation of Solomon's dilemma-assuming that the child's guardianship was determined according to responsiveness to emotional needs, and not biology-is not beyond dispute (Woodhouse, 1994, 1526). The biological parents, especially the more involved mother, gave several hints to the English Court, that the child's best interests lay with the foster mother: Though her pain at being torn away from her son moved her to disagree in the hearing to his adoption, her compassion for him is mirrored in her ambivalence. After voicing her objection, she is, at one stage, before any litigation, ready to concede to adoption if the child visits her for a month each year. If the foster mother had acted in a more caring and trust-inspiring way towards her, the litigation might have been avoided. The child finally returned to England, not because of a court order, but probably because the 'victorious' biological parents recognized he was unhappy in South Africa with them and in his community of origin.

The case illustrates the abyss between respect for the child's culture as a context of personal meaning and cultural sensitivity as commonly perceived. Using abstract notions of culture and ancestry and neglecting culture as a context of personal meaning, the court ignored the significance of the biological parents' choices. The parents identified the child's best interests as not growing up in the Zulu village of his mother. They preferred him to grow in the home of a white Afrikaner woman. Later they preferred offering him a rare opportunity to actualize his – human- potential through an English education- first in South Africa and then in England- to educating him in a Zulu environment, probably, with meager resources and limited educational opportunities. Finally, I suggest the parents were forced by the outcome of the proceedings, ignoring their hints, to take the initiative to break away from their offspring. They did this to respect the child's sense of who he is and ties that he would most like to preserve. It seems the child's painful struggle and the responsiveness of his biological parents to his suffering ensured protection of an individualized child-created identity. It is conceivable the parents' implied conception of identity is not inexorably tied to a place. Proponents of ethnocentric identity could have found fault in the parents' actions, especially if motivated by such a conception of identity.

To conclude, had the court recognized the child's right to an individualized identity as proposed here, the child's and feelings would have been given due weight in the first place. This would have allowed the court to protect an authentic child-constructed identity radically different from any clear-cut notion of Zulu or Afrikaner identity. The court could have utilized the child's input as to his identity to navigate a course between the child's wishes and the responsibilities of the different adults in his personal world. Such a course would have been in accordance with articles 5 and 12 of the Convention. Article 5 is significantly open-ended in its wording and would have enabled consideration of the responsibilities of the foster mother, undoubtedly a significant person in the child's life.

The case is, in my eyes, a classic example of the assertion that ethnic distinctions do not indicate the personal boundaries one sets between oneself and others, nor how society could respond to the child's sense of belonging. It clearly exemplifies the distinction and tension between cultural sensitivity as commonly perceived and respect for the child's individualized identity.

V Conclusion

The right to a self-constructed identity may be seen as deriving from the child's human dignity. The two cases examined here demonstrate how the proposed concept of identity can radically change the outcome of child-centered deliberations: A self-constructed identity is the product of the child's experience rather than an adult imposition or general approximations of children's experiences, wishes and feelings. Recognition of such an identity leads child law into new ground.

Children may need proactive state intervention to preserve relationships meaningful to them. These needs are not guaranteed under the Convention, which instead offers an ambiguous concept of identity. It mandates the child be educated to respect his own cultural identity and that of others. It does not mandate that this cultural identity be protected by the law or that the child's feelings be consequential to the legal definition and protection of his identity.

Proactive state protection may at times imply ensuring the survival of a distinct cultural identity through indefinite future generations, mirroring authentic aspirations of minority children. Traditional liberal theory cannot justify such measures. and indeed, theorists adhering to such an ethos, such as Kymlica (1989) and Tamir (1993), did not advocate proactive state action. The scope and substance of such state action, not discussed here, may justify further research.

Every society that is committed to human rights should see its way to granting clear and unequivocal recognition of the child's right to a self-constructed identity. For this purpose, an Optional Protocol to the Convention may be drafted. Once the right gains recognition, child law jurisprudence will have to develop the judicial tools needed to ascertain a child's authentic identity. Child law jurisprudence will have to overcome law's tendency towards the abstraction and objectification of culture while at the same time protecting the child from premature autonomy.

Re-understanding the child's right to identity has wide implications beyond those exemplified in the two cases discussed. For example, in a guardianship dispute, when the court rules on a child's exposure to different religious and cultural traditions, greater weight would have to be given to the child's wishes and feelings in order to protect his sense of belonging. Choosing between the Tender Age Test, the Primary Caretaker Test and Psychological Parenthood/Emotional Bonding Test (e.g. Gilat 2015; Sexton 1999; Eekelaar 1994, 46), it would be almost impossible not to give paramountcy to the child's emotional bonding. Greater consideration will need to be given to the preferences of a child's biological parents regarding the cultural, religious and ethnic identity of the couple who adopt their offspring, since such preferences may protect the evolving construction of an identity by the child. Open adoption would be preferred in the cases of some older children because closed adoption may infringe on the child's right to an individualized evolving identity.

I now return to the question of social engineering raised by Ward LJ in Re M (Child's Upbringing). I suggest that framing decisions concerning individual children in line with ethnocentric identity politics and purporting to correct group wrongs through court decisions relating to ties of individual children is a subtle yet dangerous form of well-meaning social engineering. Whereas affirmative action always aims to serve the interests of the individual minority child, here the child pays a price for correcting group wrongs. Such decisions often purport to express cultural sensitivity. In practice, they may perpetuate recreating insulated discrete identities competing with one another within a social arena which champions group differences and silences the child attempting to chart his way as a creator of meaning. A static conception of identity tying identity to place of birth may serve such a trend (Lavie and Swedenburg 1996) and may thus jeopardize the ties some children develop to their places of residence. These may be, for example, children of asylum seekers, children of foreign workers or children abducted by a parent from their place of birth because of abuse unrecognized in the country of origin.

Recognizing the child's experiences through the right to identity leads to legal responses to child law dilemmas, which may be more authentically compassionate towards the child. Protecting ties between a marginalized parent who has strayed from mainstream norms of child-rearing and, his child may be at odds with public sentiment typically keen to classify, marginalize and exclude some. Such protection may be authentically responsive to the child's needs. Thus, compassion towards the child may be less easily politicized.

Such legal responses may be less effective in serving the public interests of retaliation and deterrence of abusive parents. However, as exemplified through the two cases, it would be wrong to assume recognizing the child's right to an individualized identity will necessarily strengthen the legal status of biological parents. In the competition between biological parents and adoptive parents or between biological parents and foster parents, recognition of such a right would clearly undermine the centrality of blood 'ties' when these do not correspond with ties that are meaningful to the child.

CHAPTER 2

Responsiveness to Children and Law's Healing Power

I Introduction

This chapter explores law's responsiveness to children's experience. It is explained how such responsiveness is derivative of the concern for humanizing the law as expounded in Therapeutic Jurisprudence literature. Following Michael Perlin's example (2000), I utilize this literature to explore law's healing power.

The thought of Emmanuel Levinas is utilized to understand the ethical challenge for jurists, judges, and members of the helping professions to be responsive to the child's experience and how to overcome a universal tendency to deny it. The discussion demonstrates the problems and dilemmas involved in responding specifically to the child as the experiencing Other and suggests solutions that arise from an attempt to decipher Levinas's contribution using a Therapeutic Jurisprudence key, a key that aims to open up positive law, as it is implemented, to its humanity and power to heal.

II Responsiveness to Children's Suffering, Therapeutic Jurisprudence and the Path Blazed by Emmanuel Levinas

Healing the Law and Widening the Scope of Interdisciplinarity

Legal obligations to prevent or lessen children's suffering are rare. When the child is harmed and needs the state's protection, there is no systematic commitment to ensure the child does not undergo further suffering. Law often responds only retroactively to some of the harm caused to children by taking action to halt or limit it. However, as explained, it does not ensure responsiveness to the child as a whole person with an identity and a sense of belonging to a family and a community.

Therapeutic Jurisprudence literature explores law's capacity to be psychologically healing for individuals and relationships. It has already made extensive use of empirical findings and theoretical insights advance the well-being of children and their families through the legal system (Gal and Shidlo-Hezroni 2011; King and Tatascior 2006; Daicoff 2000; Anderer and Glass 2000). Through

 | DOI 10.1163/9789004223677_003

allowing the law to heal, Therapeutic Jurisprudence heals the law of its alienation to human experience. It is therefore, possible to view this chapter as an addition to an existing body of knowledge which, through legal provisions, rulings, and proceedings, could promote the child's well-being (Perlin, 2000; Wexler 2000). Gradual changes in the law's systemic functioning, inspired by this literature, have been taking place in various legal systems. They offer cause for optimism in this field.

This literature is directed primarily toward the social sciences. It discloses and actualizes law's human dimension. It makes sure we do not lose sight of law's potential humaneness while we engage in the complicated effort to protect procedural and substantive rights (Dauer 2000).

At the same time, there is a striking emphasis in Therapeutic Jurisprudence literature on applicability and pragmatism and a distancing from abstract deliberations, which are remote from the daily routine of the law (Wexler 2000; Stolle 2000).

In contrast, the writing of Emmanuel Levinas is philosophical; it does not deal primarily with the research literature in the social sciences or law and yet it is not detached from human emotional life and from the wealth and complexity of real life, which at times defies philosophers' rationality (Levinas 1997).

In this chapter, I shall try to bridge two complementary modes of relating to human suffering. In this effort, I am joining a growing trend in interdisciplinary writing that offers opportunities for reciprocal enrichment of the various fields of knowledge (Davidovitch and Alberstein 2008, 521).

Almost all of us suffer at times. Children, who are not subject to abuse or neglect, as these are legally defined, also suffer. I do not limit my discussion here to a particular group of children. It is relevant to all children.

My choice to focus on children's suffering is inevitably a value-laden and political choice. There will always be groups that are to some degree invisible and unheard. Thus, there will always be room for activity for a new generation of human rights advocates and activists who will identify the excluded of the next generation (Minow 1990).

Yet this does not absolve me of my duty to explicate my politics of empathy.

I have chosen to use this chapter to shine a beam of empathy on children above all others. My effort may empower children both legally and socially (Wexler 2000).

Why then have I done this?

Children are unique in several ways: They are not eligible to cast a vote or to be elected. They are almost without any political power. They have limited legal competency and are therefore lacking in economic power. Their characteristic emotional dependence on their parents is unique in its intensity (Ronen 2005a, 617–638; Freeman 1997). This is, in essence, my reasoning for what is inevitably a value laden choice.

Emmanuel Levinas dealt first and foremost with the ethical attitude which is needed for hearing the voice of the Other. His writings therefore have great relevance to the question of legal responsiveness to the child's suffering.

In the first chapter, I reasoned my position that holds children's rights discourse is at risk of becoming abstract, doctrinal and alienated from the experiences of children. The pedantic, technical adherence of some child advocates to implementing children's rights provisions in law as the professedly ultimate expression of a commitment to these children bolsters this conclusion. However, even after having characterized the discourse on children as potentially abstract, doctrinal and alienated, I do not see this outcome as inevitable or unrectifiable.

My characterization of children's rights discourse and my objective of rectifying it deeply resonate with the concerns of therapeutic jurisprudence. This jurisprudence offers a solution to the crises of purpose which legal professionals grapple with: How might the humane objectives of law and lawyering be returned, from being abstractions that drive public policy to become the daily rewards of lawyers and their clients? (Wexler 2000; Perlin, 2000).

Levinas offers us a new quality of discourse, one of genuine responsiveness. Thus, it cannot be objectively determined in terms of conventional identity discourses (Fagenblat 2010) or identity politics. Through responding the individual self-constructing his identity defines who he is an ethical subject (Fagenblat 2010). Though Levinas's call of the Other is generated by a philosophy of Judaism it is a call open to all, a call with a universal appeal. Levinas's Judaism goes beyond conventional identity politics of being Jewish as opposed to being gentile. His writing is an invitation to all who are willing to take on responsibility of the Other. He is passionate about making a contribution to present-day ethics. Only the individual can decide what it means to be a responsive human being at the juncture he is in. Thus, Levinas expresses a concern with both avoiding tribalism and a facile return to a universality of uniformity (Hammerschlag 2010).

My proposal for protection of a self-constructed identify founded on a commitment to multiculturalism as presented at the outset of this essay can be seen as consonant with Levinas's position. In this chapter, following the path blazed by Levinas, I hope to contribute to law's responsiveness to children's suffering thus contributing to a child-centered therapeutic jurisprudence.

In Chapter 1 rejected replacing the notion of a 'normal' identity with the endorsement of ethnocentrism associated with identity politics. I explained how rejecting ethnocentrism may lessen the exploitation of identity politics to promote community interests at the individual's expense. Here, following Levinas, I move another step further from conventional identity politics (Fagenblat 2010). I extricate an ethical call generated by a philosophy of Judaism from from its ethnic origin. I am concerned with elucidating the vocation it offers all who are willing to meet the responsibility it entails.

Levinas 's rejection of identity politics invites us to transcend a preoccupation with justice for ourselves. It invites us to be good and generous to the Other through responsiveness to his unique identity, though he may not be in a position to benefit us. Burggraeve's discussion elucidates this:

> Human rights do not merely begin from just society, but also transcend it. Those of us who think and act according to our call to promote human rights, thus for example standing up for the rights of the marginal and alienated, in fact do more for humanity than could any socio-political structure in itself, since such structures are by definition immune to a sense of the unique identity of each other.
>
> BURGGRAEVE 2007, 182

What is suffering?

I use suffering here to mean a burden of anxieties, troubles, torments or discomfort (Webster 1996, 1421). Suffering, thus defined is always subjective, always an experience.

This includes suffering caused to a young offender who has been punished for his offense – a youth who has been exploited during his childhood and during his development exploited others as he has been exploited. It includes suffering caused to a parent who has been ruled to be unsuitable to care for his child following an addiction to drugs, or whose child has been adopted against his will. It also includes the suffering of an empathic judge who is required to make decisions, which cause suffering to others. Robert Cover, in his classic work 'Violence and the Word', to which we shall return, sheds light on how the suffering of those subjected to legal decisions always remains, to some degree, distant and unreal, a suffering which we cannot share fully (Cover 1998, 238). We can always aim to make the Other's suffering more and more real.

What I have explained so far cannot nullify the moral imperative to protect a child from harm that is not experienced as such by the child. Not every abuse causes suffering, and that is fortunate. Thus, for example, a three-year-old child is harmed by sexual abuse though he may experience no suffering and a nine-year-old is harmed when we deny him free education, although he may enjoy remaining at home with his parents.

In this way, the legal system ensures that children are given the right to free education, the right to the integrity of their person, and many other rights. However, at the same time, it does not respond to children's suffering in countless instances.

As mentioned, the purpose of this chapter is to examine the background of the law's failure to be responsive to children's suffering and to propose how to rectify this state of affairs. Therapeutic Jurisprudence searches for solutions that serve the emotional well-being of the individual but does not attempt to trump individual rights (Stolle 2000).

Here too I do not envision detracting from the scope of child protection under law in situations where the child did not experience suffering. I clarify the nature of protection needed in situations where suffering is present. I do not suggest concern for the emotional well-being of the child as a justification for trumping rights.

The title of this chapter is based on the linguistic distinction between responsiveness to others' suffering and reaction to this suffering.

What distinguishes reaction from responsiveness? Reaction is an effort to solve a problem by an observer who views the incident as a disturbance. Reaction is not an effort to draw emotionally closer to the Other's suffering, and even less is there an attempt to place one's self in the affected person's shoes, to feel his suffering and acknowledge it so it can be cured or relieved.

Responsiveness both sees the pain in an objective way which is detached from a personal viewpoint and also hears a distinct voice which we allow to enter the observer's consciousness.

As an example, when a child cries, and I try to comfort him, I recognize suffering and try to respond to it through offering comfort. If I calm a crying child to silence the crying, I am reacting to a disturbing noise without responding to suffering the child may be expressing in his crying. Suppose the child has been insulted, and therefore, cries and angrily demands chocolate as compensation. I could give him chocolate without taking interest in his suffering, or I could respond to his suffering without giving him chocolate. This example also demonstrates the difference between responsiveness and sentimentality.

I cannot focus on the Other's suffering without seeing with my own eyes the person facing me, and this vision cannot be anything other than subjective.

Responsiveness and Responsibility

By responding to the Other, I am forever transformed. Through responding to the Other I reconstruct my own identity. Levinas illustrates this through opposing Ulysses return to his island with Abraham's journey to the unknown with no possibility of return to his land of birth. Abraham, through accepting the vocation of responsibility for the Other is for ever changed. He can never return to who he was. Ulysses on the other hand returns to the solace of the familiar. Both his origin and destination are known to him.

Levinas invites us to a journey which transcends a return to the past and an actualization of fully known destiny, he invites us to abandoning our ego satisfied with a constructed unchangeable identity (Tahmasebi-Birgani 2014; Levinas 2004).

Levinas explains that seeing the person facing me is an experience which has ethical significance. This significance is because of its potential for my responding to his suffering, and a potential for my assuming responsibility towards him. Human connectivity, as Levinas and others describe it, is based on the absence of apathy towards the Other. It is based on a willingness to open up to him, and this leads to a responsibility which is not dependent on reciprocity (Levinas 1988, 156–165; Connolly 1996; Minow 1996, 279–282; Kleinman 1996, 287–290; Minow 1991, 1665; Slonim-Nevo and Lander 2008; 2001, 18; Levinas 1990c, 151–153).

Because legal responsibility is, by its very nature, limited, the ethical challenge of deciding how the law should respond to the Other is of particular interest and importance (Anderson 2006, 190–191 and 199–200).

According to Levinas, real responsibility for the Other goes beyond my interests, or 'our interests', and beyond personal considerations. When I am ethically responsible for the child's well-being, I am not responsible only up to a certain limit. I do not cease to be responsible when 'it doesn't pay for me', since the very consideration of responsibility in utilitarian terms, including the expectation of reciprocal benefit, is anchored in a social contract which is 'a lack of responsibility' in the ethical sense.

Orange clarifies the nature of the responsiveness which brings about responsibility for the Other:

> When one loves someone one does not feel obliged, as Levinas said. Surely this is true, but Levinas was speaking not of intimate and personal relationships but rather of the widow, the orphan and the stranger. He was speaking of the neighbor whom I watch taken away to the concentration camps.
>
> ORANGE 2011, 59

Responsiveness to an ethical challenge through law allows us to safeguard the ethical nature of legal responsibility anchored in positive law. It offers legal responsibility a profound, existential humanity; it offers some kind of partial response to the yearning for justice and can makes the law more healing.

Ethical responsibility for the Other creates an opening for ending estrangement from the Other and creating a human bond with him. It does so through challenging jurists to overcome the temptation of comfortable, smug respect for the formal rule of law. An uneasy look at the discrepancy between what legal rules typically offer and what we need to do in order to genuinely respond to the suffering of real people could lead us to change our aims. The Levinas-eque view of the law could, therefore, contribute to law that is more therapeutic in better serving the psychological well-being of the Other.

Levinas challenges the extreme individualism which promotes individual rights over personal responsibility. Such a challenge has a place within human rights theory and practice.

I see Levinas as a passionate human rights advocate in his own way. Levinas' challenges subjugation of the Other, a subjugation to which we expose the Other when we are not committed to his human rights. Such subjugation is an expression of egocentrism, which Levinas proposes we transcended. He suggests that we are all responsible for the Other (Burggraeve 2002) and this cannot but include the child as Other.

Levinas proposes a paradoxical approach in which I find myself within the Other, and I realize myself through a commitment to the Other. At the same time, I and the Other remain separate from each other, human beings with individual rights worthy of respect and protection.

III Is There a Cure to the Universal Phenomenon of Denying Children's Suffering?

Denial of Suffering as a Tool to Preserve the Status Quo

Martha Minow (1991, 283) offers a parable. To paraphrase her: A rich man is enjoying a lavish banquet held at his home when from his window, he spots an old woman, half-starved and weeping, approaching his door. Feeling a rising pity in his heart, he calls over his servant and tells him: "This woman is breaking my heart! Banish her". The parable is clear. Repressing suffering from our consciousness helps us deny its existence. 'Successful' denial allows us to avoid placidly social change. Each person is enveloped in his own private world and feels absolved of all responsibility. The lives of the people living alongside him could be devastated, so long as the material world, in our days the technological world, continues to protect him and serve his needs. This sort of existence and behavior has been described as 'existential blindness' (Lewis 1998, 55–61).

Jeffrey Bloechl explains the psychological dynamic in light of Levinas's thought:

> Levinas has no trouble with the notion that the same point at which he detects the institution of radical responsibility can also adjourn to profound evil. On the other hand, both that responsibility and its extreme perversion seem to confront us at the height of self-awareness, when a neighbor's face singles us out as One–for–the–Other. Your face can awaken me to a responsibility beyond any meaning I may give to it, or it can can awaken in me a morbid desire which consumes every investment I may make in this world, including in our relation. What distinguishes these two paths? Whereas perversion is an already operative form of referring everything to oneself, what Levinas sometimes calls the "metaphysical desire" for the Good points infinitely beyond being and possession.
>
> BLOECHL 2000, 143

Those who embrace an alienated approach blind themselves to repression, which typically exposes children to abuse and victimization. Blindness allows them to continue with their lives without interruption.

So is there a cure?

Many who are not characterized as law breakers, or who are not diagnosed as being mentally ill, are still capable of witnessing the brutal beating, abuse, and degradation of children, and still fail to do a thing to save them (Cohen 2001, 69–74). Witnessing 'intolerable' suffering, especially when the observer did not initiate the suffering, may cause building psychological defenses in the observer's psyche that are more sophisticated and impermeable than those in existence before the experience. Thus, the very act of facing firsthand suffering is not enough to prevent an alienated response. It may even reinforce it.

However, facing suffering- while focusing on the sufferers' point of view and stressing his suffering- has at times cured this blindness (Gandhi 1994; Mandela 2002; Harris 2001, 288–293).

Mental preparation is needed. We need to do more than simply read legal precedents. We need to do what will open up our minds to the ethical horizons of the law.

A lack of responsiveness may at times express a natural human difficulty in witnessing suffering (Wexler 2000; Dauer 2000; Stolle 2000). Thus, we hear about those who avoid visiting Third-World countries, where children's suffering is exposed on the streets. We hear of those who brake contact with a friend or family member because of the disgraceful way they treat their children. Those who avoid a trip or a relationship with a friend to avoid facing human suffering, but who do not try to repress their awareness of that suffering are not indifferent towards this suffering, although they are not doing anything to respond to the suffering or to offer relief.

Abstaining from trips or relationships with a friend or family member as a way to exclude children's suffering from one's consciousness is not enough. Children's suffering may challenge our peace of mind. The media is filled with information about it. Despite that, most of those exposed to this information shut themselves off psychologically and deceive themselves into doing nothing. The bystanders convince themselves that it is not their problem, either because they cannot identify with the sufferers, or because they believe they cannot do anything to stop the suffering (Cover 1998, 238).

Responsiveness to children's suffering is a political act in the sense that it alters the basic order of society. Irresponsiveness does not always stem from subconscious denial. Many have an interest in silencing and repressing the voice of suffering children, since they perceive this repression and silencing as serving their own interests. They may do this both because they benefit from the current existing order, and because their self-confidence and peace of mind depend on their public image, which is threatened by such voices (Levinas 1997, 153–162, and 255; Ronen and Ben Harush 2005, 207 and 239–246; Connolly 1996).

'Injustice', 'evil', as experienced by those same children and the people who are significant to them, are perceived by some professionals – both jurists and non-jurists – as little more than expressing the individual problem of those who are experiencing and speaking about these things. Therefore, forms of discourse continue to exist and develop, which do not translate the voice of suffering into an ethical claim for legal responsiveness. In this way, the language of ethical claims which is used by the Other is 'cleansed' of the ethical challenge rooted in it, and remains only as a testimony to the problems of the Other. Thus, for example, the pornography of personal experience, which is common in the media, allows sentimentally invading the privacy of a single-parent family whose children are hungry for food because the mother lost her job, without offering redress to the family and its members or identifying social ills that brought about this suffering.

This is true even when the law is the direct cause for this suffering. Personal, emotional, distressed talk about the injustice done to a family or about public apathy is often left disconnected from anchors in current professional legal discourse. This discourse cannot be characterized as a healing discourse, though therapeutic jurisprudence has paved the way to make law more healing (Perlin, 2000, Dauer 2000; Wexler 2000; Stolle 2000).

In this way, the failure to recognize the law's ethical horizons persists, horizons which Levinas has pointed out. The compassion aroused by suffering is not translated into ethical conclusions or legal substance, and we can therefore understand those who say it is not compassion that they want but rights.

Compassion does not necessarily precede recognizing rights. It may be a cheap replacement for such recognition.

A therapeutic jurisprudence outlook has already started to show that rights and well-being concerns do not have to negate each other |(Wexler 2000, 452). In this recognition, I find support for my position that we do not have to choose between respecting the human rights of the Other and responding to his suffering compassionately. Respect for human rights can be a form of compassionate responsiveness.

Legislation and court rulings on child protection typically focus on the intimate family space and abstain from recognizing systemic societal ills that cause personal suffering. They also typically fail to recognize how such ills contribute to the inability of families to protect their children and to act in their interests. (Ronen 2008a; Roberts 1999; Cahn 1999; Olsen 1985; Wright 1998; Schorr 1993; Guggenheim 2000; Brooks and Ronen 2006; Ronen 2008b).

These acts of legislation and rulings are nourished by public discourse, and they in turn feed into the discourse. This reciprocity gives rise to hope. It is possible to affect law's responsiveness to children's suffering through a public discourse. A judicial or legislative statement can empower the excluded and achieve public legitimacy for their voices. These voices tell of suffering, of being robbed of the ability to be heard and of their credibility.

How, therefore, can mental preparation take place for the meeting with the Other which will open the mind of the observer, listener or reader to the ethical horizons of the law?

The boundaries between 'us' and the 'them' shape the limits of legal commitment to preventing suffering, yet these boundaries do not have to remain static. As individuals and as a society, we may see these boundaries as an invitation to continually expand our awareness of inequity to the Other and to overcome a sense of threat when facing differences. If we see 'otherness' as a commandment to care for the Other and thus respect their human rights, for example, through the universally recognized Golden Rule, we become less alienated from them. We may be moving through a gradual process of widening the scope of our empathic responsiveness. We may extend our responsiveness at first directed to family and close friends, to include our extended family, our community, our ethnic group and eventually all humanity.

We can hope to achieve responsiveness every person's suffering based on our common humanity. As explained in Chapter 1, identity can become grow to become dynamic and inclusive; the boundaries of solidarity can be expanded. As explained there, classic portrayals of such an evolutionary process of changing identifications may be found in the meditations and actions of leaders of our age such as Mahatma Gandhi and Nelson Mandela.

According to Levinas, denying the Other's suffering begins with a an intellectual approach that is divorced from one's experience of the Other. Seen through the prism of a detached alienated intellect, suffering becomes abstract, a statistic, a bureaucratic matter. Levinas writes that there are tears which a civil servant cannot respond to as a civil servant (Levinas 1996, 23) and yet despite that, he believes the state and its emissaries cannot allow themselves the privilege of remaining indifferent to human suffering. How do these realities co-exist? The identification of the civil servant with his role prevents him from being able to respond through prevailing norms he implements to the suffering with which he is confronted. Denial of suffering makes it easier for the system to function, but just because the civil servant cannot show understanding for tears in his official role does not mean that he cannot see them at all (Alford 2007, 114–118).

Experiencing the suffering of the Other may radically influence our personal ethics and sense of justice. Such an experience may be sublimated into a potent driving force for change, one that can radically change the social order (see also Erikson 1970):

> Even when the civil servant cannot respond as such, he can open up emotionally and respond as a human being, as an ethical subject, to the tears caused by the functioning – even the reasonable functioning – of the bureaucratic hierarchy which is subordinate to legal norms. Indeed, the public servant, and this includes the judge or social policy maker, cannot and should not devote himself completely to the endless needs and demands of the Other, since there is a third party, an entire public which is competing for the limited resources. The public servant, too, has legitimate needs and wants. He, too, has a personal life to which he hopes to return, physically and emotionally, at the end of a workday. The lack of responsiveness offered under existing laws in light of the infinite number of other individuals who need to be served creates constructive tension. Such tension can lead to ongoing development of the legal rules alongside an uneasy, reflective, application of the existing rules. The alternative to this tension is blind loyalty to the existing order which is symbolized by the state and the rule of law in its narrow, formal sense. This loyalty is conceptualized by Levinas as idolatry, a loyalty which fails to measure up to the responsibility and challenge of being a citizen of a democracy.
>
> LEVINAS 1997

Levinas experienced the most extreme form of loyalty to the State in the 20th century, Hitlerian ideology, as a Jewish French prisoner of war in Nazi Germany

(Levinas 1997, 291–292). Nazi Germany which Levinas experienced originated from a democracy (the Weimar republic). Levinas could therefore be saying that Nazi rule exemplifies a failure to measure up to the personal responsibility by millions of German former Weimar republic citizens.

A loyalty to a democratic state which does not bind one to the social order is a tool to building up responsibility towards the Other. It seeks to use the unremitting tension among competing demands of Others. It aims to reach generalizations, which take everyone into account.

This approach can include those who are close to me at any given point in time, and third parties, millions of others, who are further away at that point. We must study the ties to others whom we face and evaluate. Through ongoing dialogue with others whom we meet, we can reach an increasingly nuanced balance between various competing demands, a balance which can be termed social justice. Thus, for example, I, an Israeli Jewish man, face both middle-class Jewish children but also the children of immigrants, both Jewish and non-Jewish and the children of Arab Israelis and Palestinians. Jews have been subject to thousand years of persecution. As a man of faith, I fully agree with Jeremy Rosen that this fact does not justify blindness to the suffering of Others and that such blindness is betrayal of our Creator (Rosen 2005a, 41). Through ongoing dialogues with the Others in my world, I may become able to do more than I had previously thought possible (see Burggraeve 2002, 135–137). Thus, I may become able to balance out unique demands and to transform the law, which creates general norms, into something more responsive, more therapeutic, more healing.

Burggraeve explains how Levinas's call for responsibility and responsiveness transforms the underlying ethos of human rights through a reciprocity that is not self-centered:

> My responsibility is total and inalienable. But, 'thanks to God', I am not alone: there are Others who also have their own responsibility, as radical as mine. 'Fortunately', I too fall under the responsibility of Others both near and far. Hence there is a communal space of identity and reciprocity in which I and the Others all partake, in which I and the Others are counted together, and where as a citizen, I have as many common, ordered rights and duties as does anyone else. On the level of the unique Other, I am uniquely responsible, but on the level of the third I am also an Other for the Other: the original and derived asymmetry becomes a derived symmetry. This also marks the reemergence of human rights and the right to freedom They are no longer the expression of merciless

> self-interest, but the realization of reciprocal recognition of one another's equality and autonomy as deserving respect.
>
> BURGGRAEVE 2007, 141–142

In theory and practice, the uniqueness of the Other does not rule out the possibility of universalizing his demands and of balancing between these and the unique demands of other people with whom he lives. When we examine social life, even without reference to Levinas' reflections, it is easy to understand that ethical norms, including legal norms in child law, are shaped not only by theorists in the context of abstract professional discourse – although there are those who believe that this is how the laws should be shaped (Kleinman 1996, 288). Such norms are also shaped in the public arena, where the individual case, the personal experience, the human narrative, has, a central role, though this role is hidden and often denied (Brooks and Ronen 2006; Minow 1991, 1665; Delgado 1989).

Turning theoretical attention to responsiveness to the child's suffering can ensure that shaping child law will not take place solely within the arena of abstract professional discourse.

This redirection of theoretical attention can increase awareness of the opportunity to promote justice, through deciding between competitive ethical demands of individuals. The decision maker thus sees himself as responsible for such individuals despite their otherness or foreignness (Levinas 1988, 165; Levinas 2001; Sheehan 2000).

Of cause, I do not contend that we can protect children from all forms of suffering. There is unavoidable suffering. Examples of such suffering range from the death of his aged grandfather to a Tsunami storm which destroys the child's home (Connolly 1996).

The legal system is also bound to cause unavoidable suffering to the individual, as has been clarified by Cover in his classic work 'Violence and the Word' (Cover 1998), mentioned earlier in this chapter.

It is comfortable and therefore tempting to attribute to Robert Cover more than he has written, to convert the descriptive into the prescriptive, the deterministic or the predetermined and to see the extent of widespread alienation among the objects of the law and its creators and enforcers as a reality which should not or cannot be changed.

Translating Responsiveness into Legal Norms

Therapeutic Jurisprudence literature fundamentally challenges such a mindset. This literature, primarily in the social sciences, shows again and again how the law can be responsive to the psychological well-being of individuals influenced by the law.

Crossing the invisible social sciences – humanities divide, I have attempted to learn from Levinas' ethical outlook on the law and tie my learning to the therapeutic jurisprudence's aim of humanizing law.

In the footsteps of Levinas, we seek to create closeness where there is usually distance, a distance which is sharply exposed in Cover's paper. Levinas maintains that the ultimate closeness is that of parent and child, because it opens the 'me' to the endless possibilities of change through the Other because of being responsive to the Other.

The endless possibilities reflect the infinite differences between people, and the bond between parent and child can reveal the enormous potential in being responsive to one's fellow man (Levinas 2003). In relating to a child, we find the ethical challenge of relating to the Other in a responsive way at its climax (Ben-Pazi 2008, 274). Compassionate responsiveness to the child is compassion towards the Other whose development and adult behavior you cannot predict (Ben-Pazi 2008, 276).

I maintain that this insight by Levinas has legal implications: The state metaphorically steps into the parent's shoes when they cannot fully respond to the child's needs (Goldstein et al. 1996), in Latin 'Legalese' it is acting as *Parens Patriae*. We are therefore justified in aiming correspondingly for the responsiveness we would expect from a parent.

Through Cover's (1998) classic paper we become acutely aware that some suffering is inevitable. Thus, the need arises to examine whether and to what extent the law has responded to the child's suffering.

Returning to what is comfortable and tempting in light of this paper: There is the danger of sinking into complacency based on the unproven premise that nothing can be done, that the law is too crude a tool to respond to suffering, and that it cannot provide any remedy. This danger grows in an individualistic and sectarian society in which the temptations increase, to become alienated from the Other and to socially exclude him (Minow 1991, 285; Levinas 1988, 165). While exercising discretion in implementing and interpreting the law is bound to cause inevitable suffering, compassion, which seeks to respond to the Other's suffering might be reflected in such discretion, thereby lessening unnecessary suffering. Our stance, following Levinas, is that one must recognize the duty to have a compassionate approach anchored in law. This is an unwritten ethical duty which precedes the law. It is written in the body of the suffering person, and deciphering this 'writing' is of the beginning of compassion. Thus, for example, children who were exposed to severe emotional abuse were saved from a future of conflict with the law or mental disability when they were supported by compassionate witnesses who recognized their suffering and the injustice done to them for what they were (Cutler 1994, 11–18 and 266–269; Winnicott 1985).

Helping professionals – including jurists in formal roles such as juvenile court and family court judges, prosecutors and child attorneys – can be supportive witnesses for the children who confront widespread social denial of children's suffering, even when public awareness finds it difficult to digest the reality of children's suffering, and even when not all courts acknowledge the different forms of child abuse. However, when people significant to the child know of his suffering, or suspect that he is abused and don't act, the child may feel betrayed and abandoned (Cohen 2001, 17).

Even legal proceedings which fail to protect the child can at times be more healing to the child than the experience of dismissal of his suffering because of evidentiary considerations. If the child experiences supportive witnessing and responsiveness, the mere effort on his behalf can be reaffirming and thus valuable to him.

Levinas' work shows how discretion in interpreting and applying the law could transcend the cruelty which is built-in to blind obedience to the rational order found in legal rules (Levinas 1990c). This can be achieved without replacing the existing order with arbitrariness or anarchy (Levinas 1990a; Levinas 1990c).

We can exercise such discretion recognizing that 'there is no heart without understanding, and there is no understanding without heart', as Levinas writes (Levinas 2001, 26). The rational and the emotional do not negate each other, and there is no need to renounce one or the other (Minow 1991). They can complement each other and empower us in an ongoing personal process directed at expanding the boundaries of social solidarity. Levinas, writing of the educational experience of a parent or teacher, explains that the child can be experienced as one of us and even ours and yet at the same time he does not become ours. He belongs only to himself (Ben-Pazi 2008, 265–267).

In this chapter, I have so far attempted to show how opening up to the ethical horizons of the law, may remedy the prevalent denial of the child's suffering. But what can we do beyond that?

IV How Can Protecting Children Actualize Democracy's Unique Potential?

Children are different from other disempowered groups. Not only are they absent from the centers of economic and political power, but they also do not, as a rule, have legal and economic power because of the widespread inaccurate assumption that they generally lack the competence to exercise such power. Therefore, the exclusion of their point of view from the public discourse is more extreme than the exclusion of other disempowered groups, such as cultural minorities.

This is all the truer for children who need state protection, protection that does not prevent their suffering.

A child who needs state protection is liable to be harmed because of his relative weakness both initially by individuals in his community of origin and or in protective placements and subsequently by politicians and policy makers who disrespect his fundamental rights. Such rights, anchored in the Convention, include the right to nutritional security, basic health, free elementary education, and suitable living conditions. These rights continue to suffer heavy blows in states that have ratified the Convention (Ronen and Greenbaum 2008, 1–11). It is therefore, important that the parent's protective power – even when misused – not be replaced with a state emissary's power's without safeguarding that the decision maker is accountable for being responsive to the child. Even if a professional decision maker is convinced he is committed to the child's well-being, if the child does not experience attentiveness based on respect to his experience of suffering,– despite procedures 'to protect him', laws intended 'for him', and a policy plan for 'child protection', and sometimes specifically because of these – he could internalize the message that "might makes right". This may happen in a society which considers itself as caring and child centered. Such a child is liable to 'privatize' what he experiences as state violence (Shakdiel 2001), that is, choose to be violent himself. Thus, despite well-meaning efforts, child who did not experience responsiveness may grow up to be an individual saturated with rage and violence. He may revengefully reject ethical responsibility towards the Other and become alienated from human suffering (Federle 1990; Melton 1992 and 1994).

Despite this danger, the tendency to stifle the child's voice continues. Why and how?

The notion that adults can learn something from children is still presented as ridiculous, at times. For hundreds of years, the idea has been accepted in various cultures around the world that the child is an object either of control or care and that the child's self-expression should be silenced. Recognizing the child's truth on his suffering is unnatural since there is still a prevalent tendency to justify child abuse or deny it.

Therefore, it is not only that the child's suffering continues while he is protected through law's intervention on his behalf, Normative abuse persists despite the Convention's proclamations (Walant 1995; Ronen 2006).

A father who humiliates his daughter by calling her a 'prostitute' because she allows herself to be used by men, or who humiliates his son when he calls him a 'criminal' because the son stole candy from a shop or took some change from his parents' desk, may cause the child suffering which will be denied or justified by society.

Michael Freeman clarifies how we are prone to deny the normative abuse occurring within our societies:

> When culture is discussed in the context of human rights it is easy to assume that we are talking only of cultural practices in the developing world. But this is not so. To take a simple example, it could be argued that the English cultural practice of sending children away to boarding public (really very private!) Schools is not in children's best interests. But it is not such practices upon which attention focuses. It is rather on female genital mutilation (FGM), child marriage, arranged and forced marriage, practices which tend to be prevalent in the developing world or in parts of it ...
>
> There are cultural practices which it is possible to reconcile with the best interests standard and others which fall outside any margin of appreciation. Slavery and apartheid are the clearest examples of the latter. Slavery, and practices similar to slavery such as imprisonment within brothers and forcing children into prostitution, cannot escape censure because they are endemic within certain cultures.
>
> FREEMAN 2007, 34–35

Legally recognizing these children's suffering involves narrowing the freedom of the adults who abuse them beyond what is socially acceptable. It entails calling a spade a spade – calling normative abuse – abuse. In practice, legal categories often shy away from responding to the child's suffering both within the bounds of his parental home and in state care when the abuse is socially normative.

Young offenders are a unique subgroup of children in need of protection because of their perceived threat to normative society. In the United States, the first constitutional recognition of children's rights was marked by harsh criticism of the policy of arbitrariness, which characterized the rulings in youth courts trying offenders. The Gault case exemplifies a decision which attracted sharp criticism because of the nature of the legal procedure. An adolescent who was accused of using foul language on the phone was placed in an institution for offenders. The procedure was criticized as facilitating arbitrariness, and its outcome as committing an injustice against the adolescent. This criticism forms a historic landmark in raising awareness on the rights of young offenders (Federle 1990; Melton 1994; Melton 1992; Sebba 1992).

These phenomena are the result of a situation in which the state is not obligated to ensure that young offenders on trial are being treated seriously as individuals, that their points of view are being taken seriously, and that they believe this. There is no sufficiently deep-rooted recognition that for the youths on trial, their liberty, as well as their dignity and privacy, are important (Melton 1992 and 1994).

Dismissing their point of view can be humiliating and belittling. We have begun to be recognize this through seeking to rehabilitate young offenders while involving people who are significant to them from their families and communities (Tolou-Shams, Hadley, Conrad and Brown 2012; McCamey 2010; Broeking and Peterson-Badali 2009; Malcolm 2007; Becroft 2006).

Intervention: At What Price?

Children in whose lives the state has intervened under the guise of preventing risks to their well-being form a group of children who deserve special attention, since they are at risk of silencing.

Literature examining the experiences of children who were removed from their homes because of a risk to their well-being offers evidence of the unintentional disadvantages for the children. It includes evidence of harmful interventions, disregard for the children's feelings or even for their expressed anxieties. There is little evidence of real efforts to ensure that children's feelings and wishes are understood (Kufeldt 1993).

We must create tools and suitable opportunities for children to share their hopes, as well as their suffering, with those tasked with ensuring their well-being, so that their inner truth is not dismissed unthinkingly, and so that the law realizes its power as a healing force towards them. In this field, we still have a long way to go.

Until the beginning of the 1960s, when research on child abuse first appeared, quashing discussion of the subject was backed by the theoretical view which held that children should not be believed, thereby denying their suffering (Kufeldt 1993). At times, it appears as if the era of such denial has passed, and that today society respects the credibility of children. In practice, however, there are still children who complain about abuse. The tendency not to believe them remains, and some still claim that children have hidden motives to complain.

There is a discrepancy between the readiness to believe children about injustices caused by their families and the readiness to believe them about injustices caused by the state and its emissaries. The difficulties created by this discrepancy become more severe since children naturally seek to hold on to a sense of identification with a family and a community as explained in Chapter 1, and to feel loved, and will therefore tend to take a more forgiving approach to the failings of those close to them.

Following Levinas, our answer to this troubling discrepancy is complex.

I propose that this discrepancy is preserved because of what Levinas would call a lack of maturity in approaching the state and its emissaries. We are tempted to choose between the two extremes of blind identification with the state and an all-encompassing rejection of its moral authority. Thus, we may fail to opportunity to carry out social and legal change unique to the democratic state (Levinas 1997, esp. 291–292).

Specifically, in our case, one temptation is to accept the assumption that this discrepancy is an unavoidable evil derivative of the existence of the state and its institutions. Thus, the unwillingness to believe children about injustices caused by the state and its emissaries is liable to become an expression of an unexamined creed.

An alternative temptation is to rest on our laurels after we denounce the danger of blind obedience to the state and its institutions of authority and power. Thus the readiness to believe children about such injustices may also become an expression of an unexamined creed, if it serves to justify the wholesale rejection of state protective action.

Following Levinas I suggest we transcend both temptations.

Dealing with the spiritual and moral challenge embodied in the present-day democratic state requires reflective responsiveness. We should be able to distinguish between good and evil in state actions. Blind loyalty to state action betrays the democratic state's potential.

Across-the-board reservations about the 'brute destructiveness' or 'violence' of institutional child care is also too facile a solution. These reservations belong to a class of luxuries we cannot afford if we commit ourselves to genuine responsiveness to the individual.

It could rob the child of the state's protection, even if this protection is usually the lesser of two evils and lessens the child's suffering. As Goldstein, Solnit, and Freud explained more than a generation ago, at times it is impossible to do more than 'the least detrimental alternative', a term coined by these authors: any alternative is detrimental to a degree. Every intervention by the state involves a price, but there are situations – spelled out both in their writings and elsewhere – in which the alternative, inaction, is clearly worse than action (Goldstein et al. 1996).

To sum up, there are two extreme positions, first, the justificatory position – which claims that the price of intervention is a necessary evil which cannot be changed – and second, the position which is based on an all-embracing mistrust of state actions aimed at child protection, which holds that state violence is always destructive, and is aimed at preserving the status quo.

I propose a third stance, one which acknowledges the dangers inherent in state intervention, but also the important challenge of being ready to bridle the power of the state for the good of the child. Levinas might have termed this position a Jewish revolutionary stance since it is opposed to using violence to destroy the existing order, but it also does not attribute holiness or any intrinsic value to the status quo, and it never ceases to challenge it in nonviolent ways (Levinas 1990a).

V What Should Be the Principal Aim of State Action on Behalf of the Suffering Child?

Which Takes Precedence? Justice, Truth, or Preventing Abuse?

We must first decide what should be the decisive factor in responding to the child's suffering: preventing child suffering, revealing the truth, or 'doing justice' to others?

There is nothing *conceptually* innovative in my assertion that doing justice to a powerless individual at times involves preferring to prevent harm to that individual over offering absolute justice to others. Levinas elucidates the conceptual point by reminding that to the extent that the rational order that justice embodies is balanced by compassion it is no longer absolute justice. Absolute justice is cruel justice (Levinas 2001, 26–28).

I assert, that implementing this insight in child law means that un-cruel justice allows us to prefer a helpless child's interests over considerations of absolute justice towards her parents. Thus, we may choose to lower evidentially requirements or procedural safeguards when proving harm to the child. We may prefer violating family privacy to risking continued such harm.

In practice, the paths taken by the courts for doing justice to the child are not well paved. The question of what can be defined as doing justice to the child has been answered in different ways throughout history. Awareness to the child's suffering and to moral duty to respond to it change and deepen. Thus, the answers to what is justice to the child also evolve (Nandy 1990, 32–33).

There is no consensus on the proper balance between doing justice to the child's parents and responding to the child's suffering. Following Levinas, I contend that responding to the child's suffering is, in itself, a form of justice. The choice who to be compassionate to is always a value-laden political choice. This stance calls for the conclusion that reevaling the truth through law and assigning legal consequences to this exposure is only one way of many to carry out justice. In the legal world, a different view is prevalent. The goal of uncovering 'the' truth is perceived in many instances as the ultimate expression of seeking to do justice. It is assumed there is such a thing as 'reality as it really is', which is the 'truth' the law is seeking to reveal.

Formal decisions on children's affairs are based on factual truths. However, it is not always clear *what* reality the court is attempting to reveal in the matter of children. What is the truth that it is ethically right to prove, and to what extent does selecting a truth suitable for legal attention have to be guided by the goal of protecting children from suffering, or by considerations of justice towards the child's parents? In my view, it is not enough that an exception is made in cases when revealing the truth will expose the child to risk of harm.

Revealing the values behind law's hidden choices requires an ethical discussion aimed at selecting which truths about children should be proven in court.

Let us assume that those who seek the well-being of the child are sincere in their efforts to obtain evidence of risks or harmful incidents and that they are truthful. This does not guarantee we protect the child against preventable suffering or that we can recognize other worthwhile aims for protective state intervention.

What then is the proper goal for the state to pursue? A situation in which public attention is always focused on proving a seemingly objective truth regarding child abuse is different from a situation in which public attention is focused on the significance which the child attributes to the harm, the suffering as the child experiences it.

The greater the discrepancy between the significance attributed to professional understanding of child harm and the significance attributed to the child's perception of the harm, so too is the potential suffering of the child greater because of the state intervening to protect him. This suffering reflects alienation between the child and those who seek his well-being as state emissaries.

Thus, for example, a parent who provides the child with food, clothing, and health services at the lowest objective level may be perceived by the child as a dedicated and loving parent committed to the child's well-being.

Child protection workers are liable to reject the child's perception without any hesitation. They may cite psychological distortions on the part of the child as explaining his perception and fail to give real weight to the child's experience including feelings about his own well-being (Ronen 1997, 93). How can we explain this tendency?

At times, there is in professional and popular culture an expectation of the professional to be an expert who amasses all the insights and knowledge, a person who knows what must be done and bases his opinions on objectively proven facts, such as who did what to whom and when, without asking those concerned what they feel and what they would like to be done (White 2011; Morgan 2006).

This belief in the professionals and professional knowledge is accompanied by ascribing preeminence to abstract knowledge, which does not stem from the professional's experience, nor from information from the injured party himself, coupled with a disregard of the dynamic social structuring of the definition of what constitutes abuse, neglect or harm (White 2011; Morgan 2006; Bilsky 1997, 152–153).

The direct exposure to experience envisioned by Levinas requires the observer to try to put aside his defenses and expose himself to the existence of the Other in an unprotected sphere, in order to achieve an understanding, which would lead to a view of the Other as made of 'flesh and blood', as vulnerable and exposed to suffering. Naturally, child protection professionals are interested in listening to children to discover how they were harmed, but they may be less enthusiastic about consulting children about the outcome of the proceedings to protect them. They may act on the basis of a sweeping assumption that within child protection laws giving paramountcy to the child's best interests, the state always acts in the child's best interests. Children could experience shock at the speed with which measures are taken to protect them. The sense of uncertainty and loss of control which result when this happens are expected to heighten their sense of being weakened, which is in any case a central experience of children who have been harmed (Melton 1992; Kufeldt 1993; Fortin 1998, 391).

The child's Best Interests is that he be responded to, and that his suffering be remedied. As explained in section B above, the very fact of the legal recognition of his harm could have a healing, therapeutic quality, through his experience of supportive witnessing even when the legal process as a whole may not necessarily be beneficial.

A child harmed by his kin could suffer additional harm when the harm is exposed. The accused kin may feel his dignity has been wounded and he may be rageful because of perceived betrayal.

These dangers to the child are counterbalanced by the belief the child can benefited from the very power of wide-ranging social recognition of the harm done to him and through suitable welfarist intervention.

Often enough, settling for identifying children who have been harmed and proving the harm, has caused more harm than good, when the state does not adequately treat those children after they have been identified. Professional actions that focus on providing legal proof of harm and not on repairing the abuse cannot be seen as aimed at ensuring the child's well-being as a whole person with his own wishes, feelings, and familial and communal identity. We can expect such actions to cause the child suffering (see also Davidson 1995, 359; Stevenson 1992).

Such practice is not compatible with the legal duty Convention to give due weight to the wishes and feelings of the child on all matters pertaining to him under article 12 of the Convention.

Therefore, state intervention which does not consider the child's suffering – and suffering by its very definition cannot be understood except by a close examination of the child's personal experience of it – does not justify restricting the child's liberties or those of his parents. Otherwise, we are liable to justify paternalistically one stance and then it's very opposite in the name of the child's best interests (Freeman 2007; e.g. Gilat 2015).

I therefore conclude, that proving truths about harm should not be the proper aim of state actions on behalf of the suffering child, but rather the aim should be to prevent suffering. Typically, this aim is not anchored in law.

VI How Can We Respond to the Child's Suffering through the Best Interests Principle?

From Pseudoobjectivity to Intersubjectivity

Having reasoned the position that the State should aim to prevent the child's suffering, I would now like to show how we can do this through the Best interest principle. As Kaplan (2001, 2002) explains, the prevalent conception envisions an objective decision making tool. The proposed intersubjective conception seeks to establish generalizations about the child's Best Interests derived from exploring the experiences of individuals and the adequate responses to them.

Children should receive protection against the abuse which lurks in the belief that we 'the adults/professionals/jurists/state representatives/the movement/religion or party' know what the problem is: What is the real abuse to the child, what really causes them to suffer? Often helping professions – including child attorneys and youth judges – describe the problem based on their knowledge of what is good for themselves, implicitly equating they consider as good with what is good for the child.

We are liable to forget that to ensure the Best Interests, we should examine the child's experience of harm paying attention to what various events in the child's life mean to the child. If we do neglect the child's experience, we may end up being part of the problem instead of being part of the solution.

At times, we hear a reference to the child's truth regarding his experience as the child's 'inner truth'. This may suggest a perceived discrepancy between the child's subjective truth and the subjective legal truth which is disassociated from the child's truth. I believe, the center point of the discussion on the Best Interests is how the child's truth may become legal truth, a truth which has the power to change the child's everyday life.

On Helping Professionals Overcoming the Limitations of Theoretical Knowledge

Legal regulation based only on technical principles, bureaucratic norms and abstract knowledge – including knowledge of minority cultures or of children with special needs – is inadequate. It cannot be sensitive to the complexities of the lives of children and to the methods which could contribute to their emotional well-being (Brooks and Ronen 2006).

Theoretical knowledge and individuals' knowledge on their own interests and needs must complement each other if we are to understand the individual's best interests. Otherwise, knowledge, though scientifically -based, will at best offer a pale reflection of reality, and at worst, a misleading and distorted portrayal of it (see also White 2011; Morgan 2006).

Thus, for example, the professional may have no theoretical knowledge about open adoption in a given culture. Knowledge stemming from fieldwork can complement the professional's understanding of identify and continuity in the child's life. Thus (in pursuance to our discussion in Chapter 1) through recourse to knowledge gained from children and their families by the professional, he may conclude that open adoption could ensure the child's right to a personal identity and the continuity of significant bonds.

When a professional sees the child and his family only by means of the prism of theoretical models and normative regulation, he cannot at times to distinguish what it is that makes the child and family unique, what they may respond to, and what could relieve their suffering. Thus, children may become almost inaudible, as if their views on what could help them are irrelevant to professional considerations. In reality, a professional, even if he claims to employ solely objective considerations, cannot do so. Professional discretion is not only influenced by known professional knowledge, which is the standard practice in his field, but also by theories, reflectively or unreflectively, developed by the professional. The personal theories are imbued with the professional's social and professional values (White 2011; Morgan 2006; Lichtenstein 1991, 147; Bilsky 1997, 117; Schon 1983).

Thus, ostensibly objective categories are, in reality, dependent on the professional's discretion. Different people interpret terms that describe the child as 'clean', organized' or 'neglected' in different ways and yet the professional justifies such categorizing through recourse to abstract knowledge. Therefore, we should not be surprised by the fact that social workers asked to decide whether a child should be placed outside of his parents' home did not reach a high-level consensus over the definition of the term 'abandoned' (Lichtenstein 1991, 147). Classification is never an objective process (Minow 1991, 175; Bilsky 1997, 154).

A recognition that the professional is not applying objective categories should create more openness towards the subjective viewpoint of the child regarding his membership in these categories. Considerations of the child's experience could be used as a check on the rescue fantasies held by society's emissaries, and illustrates the fictitious assumption that behaviors towards the child are marked by a single objective meaning (Goldstein 1975). Exercising the legal power contained in the law's mandate that offers state protection to a child from verbal abuse, which might be emotionally harmful to him does not match a prevalent social norm in many countries, which holds that talk not accompanied by physical or sexual abuse does not constitute real harm.

This norm may trickle down from the general public to helping professionals and they may act as if the child's subjective truth regarding the abuse he suffered does not truly exist, fearing that evidence of verbal abuse will not suffice (see also King and Trowell 1992, 91–93). Thus, the child's experience remains neglected.

Re-understanding the Best Interests of the Child

From Levinas, we glean an invitation the professional to see his encounter with the child as an encounter with the 'face' of another human being. In every human encounter, Levinas explains, the Other turns his face towards us. This engagement, even when it is violent, is a form of query, which arouses questions if only we pay attention to it. It is always up to someone to be attentive and act. Most of the time, the query is simply cataloged and becomes a statistic, which leaves us apathetic.

No institution can fulfill the roles of the individual who takes upon himself an imperative that makes him into a responsible subject. Institutions, too, are made up of individuals who are not free from personal responsibility. Professionals have a freedom of choice.

They might spend their time collecting physical evidence of abuse to convince the courts of what is commonly viewed as child abuse, whether this in the belief that they are doing their best to benefit children or out of a sense of alienation from the child's experience.

Alternatively, they may collect evidence as part of an overall effort to respond to the experience of the children before them while viewing accepted practice, legislation, and case law as only starting points, as potential targets of change and reform. As explained above, following Levinas, in a democratic state, the individual professional has the potential to have an influence over the fate of both individual children and children at large. The professional's attempt to exercise his rights and freedoms with this aim in mind signifies an awareness of the nature of the state. Levinas might happy to call it a sign of spiritual maturity.

As explained at the chapter's outset, almost all of us suffer at times. Thus, children, who are not subject to abuse or neglect as defined by either domestic or international laws, are nevertheless vulnerable and suffering. That is why in this chapter on responsiveness, it is appropriate to examine the substance of the principle 'the Best Interests of the child', which in accordance with Article 3 of the Convention, governs the affairs of all children, not only those who have been identified as being at risk. This governing principle controls not only the provisions of the Convention but also the provisions of the domestic laws of signatory states. The principle holds that other fields of law such as health law and labor law should also be governed by the law since they concern children.

Therefore, our discussion in this section goes beyond laws and the field of child protection, and has entered the field of the outermost circle of legal responsiveness to the child's experience. Following Levinas, we can conclude that the child's experience is mediated inevitably through one's subjective awareness, and the response to it is ethical and asymmetric in nature. Responsiveness to and responsibility for the child grow out of a willingness to devote oneself to the child as the Other. The child is always the Other for us, since the decision makers on children's affairs are all adults. Naturally, this responsibility cannot be based solely on utilitarian reciprocity (Bernasconi 1998).

It is suggested that a judge, legislator, or a helping professional who shape the conceptual and concrete meaning of the child's Best Interests step into the shoes of the person who is entitled to demand of them far more than a litigant may demand of anyone involved in the legal process. The child does not have to point out the personal advantage to be gained by anyone who responds to his needs and shows concern for his well-being. That is why the mental preparation needed to open the ethical horizons of the law with regard to the Best Interests principle is unusual.

In practice, often the decision maker does not try to enter the child's shoes. He naively assumes that he has the tools to take objective considerations into account regarding the child's best interests.

A clear expression of the pseudo-objectivity of the Best Interests Principle can be seen from a presentation of personal beliefs as fact-based realities. How can such 'truths' by proven? Through a reliance on 'the life experience' of judges, on 'common sense', or legal precedents. In practice, judicial life experience or common sense lead different judges to different, and at times, contradictory conclusions. Precedents can lead to contradictory conclusions.

In order for law to dignify the individual, factual legal decisions should reflect human experience. Such decisions should not blur or distort our understanding of experience through general assumptions that ignore knowledge within our close reach.

Thus, for example, in the case of Parham vs. J.R. (1979; Perry and Melton 1984; Perlin 2004), the US Supreme Court relied upon an antiquated legal proof from an English scholar Blackstone to justify the widespread assumption that the natural bonds of affection parents have for their children lead them to act in the best interests of their children, in an important decision impacting on psychiatric hospitalization. This assumption led to a decision which ruled that children should not be granted the right to be heard when their parents seek to hospitalize them in a psychiatric facility.

Rulings endorsing assumptions that ignore knowledge within our reach can be justified under present-day state of the art through recourse to a Best Interests principle which bases itself on so called 'judicial life experience' and 'common sense'.

Such assumptions are not necessarily legal fictions: one should not attribute to decision makers the intention to portray things inaccurately. Often, a decision maker believes these unproven assumptions and bases his decisions on them (Haley 1991, 894).

They could be used to rationalize denying the humanity of children, causing severe harm to their personal freedoms and privacy, and can be employed in defense of the existing social order which oppresses children (Haley 1991, 894).

Martha Minow sheds further light on this issue. She explains we tend to forget, that conceptions which appear natural to us and, which are taken for granted serve our interests rather than those of others, and that we dwarf the world into a shorthand language, which our brains, and apparently also our hearts, can comprehend. She explains this shorthand language reflects our stances, identities, what we view as being our needs. We characteristically do not see how the way which we divide the world reflects our unique experience and how we have learned from our parents to make sense of the world through classifications that served their interests (Minow 1991, 379).

Often, the individual seeks to understand the reality of the life of the child, but faces difficulties in grasping that his understanding is based on a certain point of view and the child, as Other, has a different point of view. Therefore, he does not disclose his assumptions and justify them (Minow 1991, 52, 60 and 65). Often, he does not recognize his own personal beliefs as being such.

Today, it is claimed that the term 'Child's Best Interests' is merely one of many vague terms which courts have typically failed to invest with concrete universally accepted meaning. This is despite the proclamations of the Convention (Alston 1994, 17–19).

One is tempted to hold fast to the objectivist 'common sensical' conception of the principle which might be alienated from the experience of the individual.

Loyalty to the 'simple meaning' of the Best Interests Principle as it is understood, for example, in the Convention, is an illusion. There may be many different and contradictory 'simple meanings' of this term under the provisions of law.

There is no one interpretive approach, which gives the concept a real and unchanging meaning. The reader seeking to interpret a provision is not bound by any particular historical interpretation of the text. This starting point is not enough to bring about a clear-cut formulation of the principle.

There is a core of basic needs and interests of children as human beings. These have been accorded the status of basic rights in the Convention, such as the right to life, or the right to protection against torture or cruel, inhuman, and degrading treatment. We can, however, learn even more about this truth – for example, what are the outer boundaries of the term 'torture'; does physical punishment or revoking social, economic or cultural rights constitute torture, which must be determined after monitoring of the child's experience as an individual (Ennew 1998; McBride 1998).

We suggest tracing the general from the intersubjective. The pseudo-objective in its professed purification from the personal and the subjective is at best irrelevant in shaping the legal norm. At worst, it serves to camouflage cultural imperialism, one form of which is the imperialism of a professional culture alienated to the child's culture as explained in Chapter 1.

The child's Best Interests as an aim of his rights must be broad enough to apply and justify truths that stem from the child's experiencing his own unique social and emotional world. It cannot include only the aims which authors of legal texts on the Child's Best Interests wish to realize, but also the goals which the reader of the texts considers worthy of realization, out of an empathic understanding of the child's experience. The level of universalization of the child's experience, to the extent to which the norm is derived from his experience, must change from case to case in accordance with the child's circumstances.

The Brown Ruling – A Forerunner of Therapeutic Jurisprudence?

In this section, I maintain that the work of interpretation cannot be objective and that the erroneous pronouncement of its objectivity was intended to make the craft of creative interpretation more comfortable by easing the integration of a new interpretation as a social norm while offering the public a sense of the continuity and stability of the law even when the status of the individual has been changed by this creative interpretation.

Through the Brown ruling, I will try to demonstrate this understanding of how courts may attempt to bring about legal change and its integration into the social fabric and how they can do this while remaining responsive.

The most dramatic example in legal history of the past century of reform, albeit indirect, in the status of children, is the ruling in the Brown affair (Brown v. Board of Education of Topeka 1954). The court significantly based its decision on extra-legal knowledge, about the effects of racial segregation, even though it could have been justified through recourse to the personal morality of the judges. This decision ensured, for the first time in the United States's legal history, the right of African-American children to integrated and equal education based on the 14th Amendment of the American Constitution. For ninety years, from the year 1864, when the 14th Amendment was passed, until 1954, the US Supreme Court refused to rule that separate cannot be equal, though this was the meaning of the 14th Amendment. Just four years before the Brown precedent, the court ruled that in the issue of racial segregation in schools, there was no need to reexamine the Plessy ruling, which ruled that racial segregation is compatible with the right to equality.

The Brown ruling, which many view as the single most important ruling in the Unites States, and perhaps in the entire world in the 20th century, set off a powerful social upheaval in the American South because of the new meaning given to an old term, 'equality', in the 14th Amendment to the American Constitution.

It is worth noting the decision on the Brown case was made unanimously. Certainly, had a few of the conservative judges who were expected to have identified with the segregationist stance formulated a minority opinion, this would have damaged the pseudo-objective message of continuity and stability, which can be found in the decision – but in truth, which sought to introduce a dramatic change into the lives of millions of adults and children.

The judges in the Brown case *chose* to respond to the experience of the African-Americans. They had a vision of African-Americans as human beings in the full sense of the word and with their ruling created justice, which had a therapeutic quality. This is the key to understanding the change in consciousness which the court ruling sought to affect. It is worthy highlighting: had they sought to remain aloof to this suffering, there would have been little difficulty in rejecting the petition, out of loyalty to the principle of equality as understood in the law of that time (see also Ronen 2008).

The US Supreme Court was an accomplice to this kind of alienation until the Brown ruling, and this state of affairs continued in the South even after the ruling: the Brown ruling to bring about the long-term change in a segregationist reality its authors may have envisioned (Sitbon 2008, 11; Love 2004). For me, this limited power reflects Levinas' insight mentioned earlier: it is not enough to read legal precedents to ensure responsiveness to the experience of the Other. What is needed is a commitment to a personal process which opens the reader's soul to the ethical horizons of the law. This apparently did not happen up to this day in certain segments of the American population which remained alienated to the rationale of the Brown ruling (see e.g. Hannah Jones, 2014; Love 2004).

It is suggested that the Brown decision be understood and explained primarily through responsiveness to human suffering. Responsiveness- its presence and its absence – can explain its significance and its partially missed potential to heal through the law. In this sense, it is a precursor of a therapeutic jurisprudence mindset par excellance.

Acknowledging Our Subjectivity

As explained above, there is a deep-seated tendency among decision makers, jurists included, to ignore the fact that their understanding is based on a personal and unique point of view and that the Other has a different point of view. In our case, it is the child's view that is liable to be ignored. Sophisticated reasoning may serve to rationalize preconceived notions (Delgado 1989, 2411). Even the Convention as a document formulated by adults must be constantly re-examined in order to overcome potential othering of children and silencing of their counter-narratives (see e.g. Barnes 2013).

In various cultures, understanding that is perceived as objective is ranked higher than the understanding that is perceived as subjective. Therefore, legal writings have traditionally claimed to be analytical, neutral, and lacking emotional involvement (Minow 1990).

This position seeks to give decisive weight to the meaning attributed to the child's experience as interpreted by an empathic listener, this is so even when the listener must reveal what weight his empathy has in shaping his interpretative position, thus risk that his understanding could be perceived as subjective and therefore, inferior (Minow 1990).

Can the approach proposed here lead to arbitrariness because of an empathic capacity which varies from person to person?

Possibly, in some cases. However, while empathic capacity does indeed vary from person to person, people who are emotionally healthy possess at least a minimal empathic capacity that allows them to recognize the child's experience. Empathic capacity can be developed within a legal context of asserting people's rights (Silver 1999; Wexler 2000, 452). Empathic capacity is universal, and the needs of a child and his psychological makeup are also universal. The reality of the life of a child is a subjective reality, as it is charged with a significance that makes up the child's world. But does a recognition of the subjective foundation in the interpretive process lead to a conclusion that 'anything goes', that the Best Interests can contain any meaning?

The interpreter's dependence on the child's narrative through his empathic capacity and a recognition of the subjective aspect of the interpretive process in no way gives total freedom to all the interpreter's subjective beliefs, stances and feelings (Bilsky 1997, 159–160).

Interpretation is a subjective process requiring empathy. We must therefore aspire to minimize the interpreter's subjective discretion insofar as it does not correspond to fundamental universal values.

Through empathizing with the child as Other, we can respond to his experience and justify a responsive rights regime committed to multiculturalism.

Thus we can reject both a position of cultural relativism and a sweeping denial of the subjective element in discerning what the child's Best Interests are. A relativist position misses the opportunity to distinguish between responding to the child's experience as and the position that 'anything goes' in the name of the local culture, the decision maker's values, or his religious or national affiliation.

The denial of the hidden subjectivity in professional discretion harms one's ability to deal with it and may serve to disguise a know-it-all smugness or alienated paternalism which determines the child's fate. Objectivity, science and professionalism are some of the buzzwords that can serve as guises.

Inspired by Levinas, I suggest that recognition of the intersubjectivity of the Best Interests Principle assumes a common empathic capacity and a fundamental responsibility among human beings which allows for a response to needs of the suffering child, as a suffering Other (Finley 1986, 1178).

A discourse which is based on a system of common meanings allows the shaping of norms, responsive to children as others, hereby doing justice to the child. The more humble and open-minded the decision maker, the more he is able to do justice with the child as Other, even if the universal rule derived from intersubjectivity never fully and accurately reflects unique experience (Sheehan 2000, 142).

As I explained earlier in this chapter, we can learn from Levinas that balancing the demand of the individual child for responsiveness with the demand of endless other parties is a dynamic process of integration between intellect and emotion. It is a living, breathing ongoing process of constantly drawing closer to justice, which will never be fully achieved. Infusing meaning into the Best Interests Principle, which goes from the subjective to the intersubjective to universalization, and from it to the legal rule, is an expression of this process.

VII More on Responding to the Child's Experience in a Multicultural Society

In the previous chapter, I explained that the child's sense of belonging deserves our respect even when it complex and conflictual. Children's right to identity is derivative of their human dignity and must protect the development of a self-actualizing individual who maintains ties to significant others affiliated with their culture.

Protecting Minority Identities

Building on these understandings, I would like to bring two examples to clarify my position on responsiveness to the other in in a multicultural society.

The first example is based on the case of an American girl of Hispanic origin who was sexually abused by her father (see also Korbin 1994 and 2002). The girl's mother reported the abuse to social welfare as soon as she became aware of it. Professionals interpreted the girl's responsibility of the day-to-day care of her two-year-old brother as 'role reversal' between parent and child. They asserted the child is tasked with responsibilities beyond her age. The professionals concluding that role reversal was taking place supported their position by literature pointing to a correlation between role reversal and child abuse. The treatment plan included protecting the girl from another sexual assault and relieving her of responsibility for her brother, so she could enjoy her childhood.

The child listened to the proposed treatment plan attentively until she heard that she could not take care of her brother every day as she had until then. At that stage, she burst into tears. The author of the chapter explained that caring for younger siblings is highly esteemed in the Hispanic culture to which the girl's family belongs. Friends of her age were given similar responsibilities to act as baby-sitters for their siblings as they played in multi-aged groups, with adults remaining close to provide help in caring for the smaller children. Certainly, caring for a younger brother could contribute to the girl's self-image, which had been harmed, since her culture values such behavior. Excluding the child from suitable and valued behavior in her culture is a form of secondary harm to the girl resulting from the intervention to protect her from her father. The claim, that the very fact of her caring for the younger brother is an objective piece of information, which demonstrates the unacceptable subordination of the girl to the needs of her parents, is alienated to the experience of the girl herself. It is incompatible with a commitment to multiculturalism since it does not allow for the possibility of different expressions of universal values (Raz 1998).

In Chapter 1, I explained why we should protect the cultural identity of the child interpreting culture as a context of personal significance. The proposed right to identity protects what the child sees as emotionally belonging to him.

Recognizing the experience of the child, who has been deprived of a meaningful role and responding to this experience within a legal framework will bring us closer to a future of responsiveness. Laws applying to children at risk can more and more respond to the child's vulnerability as a whole human being and we can hope for greater healing.

Protecting the right to identity may prevent suffering through protecting a personal world the child sees as belonging to him.

Legal responsiveness to suffering ensures the child will be protected from suffering even when the child cannot identify any such personal world.

The law cannot create for the child a family and a community affiliated to a culture ideally responsive to his needs or with ideal emotional capacities. However, when decision makers deny the limits of present-day child protection law they obstruct the legal change that can take place in a democratic society committed to the child's well-being and dignity. Law can be healing only to the extent we recognize the limitations of its present- day functioning. Therefore, literature exploring law's inherent limitations and advocating sensitivity to them in framing policy and practice is in essence, Therapeutic Jurisprudence literature even if it does not profess to be so. Such literature- for example the work of Goldstein, Slonit and Freud (1996) or this essay- may promote healing through law.

A legal commitment to respond to the girl's experience moves us to recognize the law cannot promise her anything but the least detrimental alternative. It ensures that decision makers will confront the price in human suffering of different alternatives they weigh.

We can learn for this vignette we can make child sensitive use of professional knowledge, such as knowledge about role reversal, if we turn our attention to the consequences of protecting the girl's multicultural identity, and the consequences of responding to her suffering.

More on Protecting a Unique Individualized Identity

Here is a second example:

Two children of the same age are sent to school wearing tattered clothes. One comes from a wealthy family who lives in an upper-middle-class neighborhood, and the second comes from a large family living in a poor neighborhood. Do these children need protection from parental neglect?

In order to understand the significance of the fact that the child is sent to school in patched clothes – and estimate whether he is liable to be taunted and humiliated by his peers – it is important to understand how childhood is characterized in the child's cultural environment.

The actual influences of various factors which could endanger the well-being of the child depend on the culture in which the child was raised. We cannot ignore the influence of cultural norms on the child's well-being, even when the relationship between harm to the child and the culture in which he lives are not thoroughly understood (Korbin 1994 and 2002).

Ignoring the unique characterizations of childhood in the culture to which the child belongs emotionally, removing the cultural prism, and keeping a monolithic view could cause harm to the child (Korbin 1994 and 2002). It is impossible to understand fully what the child's Best Interests are, unless one understands the meaning of the child's affiliation to a family and a community of a unique culture.

The attempt to shape an intercultural conception of the child's Best Interests requires an interpretation of behaviors towards children that are essentially different from one another. To succeed in this task, we must remember that the very fact that something is perceived as real invests it with real consequences. Thus, for example, when a child from a certain culture is expected by his family or community to identify a certain way of behavior as offensive the child may feel offended, even if the judge, social worker or lawyer is only seeking to protect the child. For example, if an orthodox Jewish boy covers his head with a Kippa or an observant Muslim girl covering her head with a Chador may feel offended by a rule banning head cover. They may see it as intrusively forcing him to abandon a practice of religious faith. This is so, even when legislators are certain that it will benefit them by exposing them to a 'liberating' culture, free of prejudice against women and of the 'primitive clothing' that sets individuals apart from 'enlightened society'. Liberal rhetoric can at times disguise prejudiced fanaticism.

Rhona Schuz's (2015) innovative discussion of attempts to ban male circumcision through misusing liberal children's rights rhetoric exemplify the problematics discussed here.

How May We Implement Our Understandings?

In the first example, when a girl who was sexually abused, was charged with care of her two-year-old brother, a virtual 'red light' would justifiably go on- role reversal possibly indicating child abuse should be *considered*. Then, a closer reading of the girl's *experience* of looking after her brother could reveal a social reality in which such caregiving is normative within her community of origin (See also Korbin 1994 and 2002).

As for the second example, we can consider the reaction needed for dealing with a situation where a child is sent to school in patched clothing by relying on our ability for empathy. Aided by our empathic capacity when exposed to the Other in all of his distinctness, we can understand the subjective experience of the children in wealth and in distress. A child from a poor neighborhood sent to school in patched clothing could suffer if his parents are rebuked and humiliated for behavior, which is normative for children and parents in his community, even though he deserves appropriate clothing no less than any other child, and even though state intervention will ensure him such clothing. The second child from the upper-middle-class neighborhood could suffer if his educators ignore the mockery he must endure for wearing these clothes to school. A third child, also from the wealthy neighborhood, might suffer if the educational and welfare authorities do not give proper consideration to the sense of partnership the child feels with his father, who is trying to function normally despite the emotional crisis his wife is undergoing.

Various pieces of factual information should set off alarm bells, but not every alarm bell has to lead to intervention. This requires a firsthand understanding of the human reality which gives rise to such facts.

VIII Conclusion

There is an abyss between the call for humanizing law that arises both from therapeutic jurisprudence and Levinasque literature and the violence, cynicism, and alienation, which pervade everyday life. Therefore, we may be tempted to view the position explicated here, one that aims to draw strength from both streams of literature in order to promote this call' s implementation, as unrealistic, utopian, or extremist. Despite this, it seems the ground has been prepared today, more than ever before, for legal responsiveness to individual experience. We are becoming increasingly aware of how humanly costly is the alienated functioning of the law, jurists, social activists and human rights advocates.

Kunz puts the choice we can make, the juncture we are at, in a wider cultural context resorting to Levinas's call for ethical responsibility towards the Other. He highlights the power we have in choosing not to resign to the prevalent cynicism:

> While psychology has moved self-interest to the heart of its philosophical assumptions about the nature of the human, self-righteous self-interest has become the heart of cynicism. Ideological self-righteousness has infected psychological, political and economic structures, as well as their respective sciences, and has thus contributed to the social disease of postmodern cynicism ...
>
> Because of our modern personal and social poverty of ethical responsibility, Levinas's philosophy, which is more radical than any ethics of personal generosity, may seem extravagant to our eyes and ears ...
>
> Being at the end of modernism but not yet established to have its own name, postmodernism has a choice between either deeper cynicism or higher hope founded on the ethical responsibility of radical altruism.
>
> KUNZ 1998, XVI–XVIII, XX

I assert, that the passage of time since Kunz pointed to our choice has only made it more acute and urgent.

I began the discussion with a reference to the lack of responsiveness to the child's experience, explaining why her unique vulnerability justifies special attentiveness to her aimed at rectifying this situation.

Following Levinas, I elucidated the concept of responsiveness along with the ethical challenge posed by the experiencing Other. I proceeded with suggesting how we may remedy universal denial of children's suffering through state action.

Elucidating law's relationship to truths which by their very nature cause the child suffering led to me to explain my commitment to legal interpretation empathic to the child without losing sight of Others involved. I explained that the denial of the subjectivity contained in judicial discretion could be used to disguise opinionated smugness and alienated paternalism.

In contrast, my proposal to recognize an intersubjective shaping of the child's Best -Interests allows for a respectful responsiveness to the needs of the child as an experiencing Other. This is so, although a universal rule derived from intersubjectivity will never fully and accurately reflect individual experience.

What constitutes invalid discrimination against the child? What constitutes humiliation and disgrace of the child? What is the legal relevance of behavior, which seems to consent to an intimate relationship in which a vulnerable adolescent is humiliated by an adult? Mainly, through analogies with other excluded groups, we are being given more and more opportunities to realize that the response given to such questions both within the legal world and outside it are not derived from objective categories, but are subject to a continuous process of growing responsiveness to the Other and to otherness within us.

I dare hope that the voice of the child as a unique individual will be more listened to and granted greater normative weight in both legal and public discourses.

I would like conclude this chapter by summarily pointing to avenues for realizing law's healing potential:

1. To fully utilize the potential of legal responsiveness to the child's suffering, we must overcome the universal tendency to deny this suffering.
2. Opening one's self to the child's suffering, the opposite of denying this suffering, is made possible through a personal, gradual psychological process. This deepens one's empathic capacity which begins with an empathic approach to the children close to us and may grow stronger until one experience empathy for the Other's child based on our common humanity. To optimize this process, the responding individual must overcome the prevalent polarization in the legal world between intellect and emotion. Emotional responsiveness to private suffering contributes to an ongoing development of the legal rules anchored in a rational order.
3. Inspired by Levinas I suggest that both viewing the price exacted for involuntary protective intervention as a always necessary and viewing it as always detrimental express immature democratic citizenship. Reflective action which distinguishes between good and detrimental in such interventions enables us to actualize democracy's spiritual challenge to us.
4. It is not enough that child protection laws ensure that detection of harm its proof and effective halt. The aim of child protection must be to prevent the child's suffering as a whole person. We need to be respectfully open to her views and feelings and to her sense of belonging to a family and a community.
5. The Best Interests principle should be founded on a quest for intersubjectivity: Attempts at generalization based on responsiveness to the subjective suffering of different unique individuals can lead to the framing if a worthy universal norm defining the Best Interests of the Child as a principle governing the interpretation of children's rights.

Through these interim conclusions, readers are invited to join a journey which we are only beginning. I suggest we let go of present-day children's images and become open to their reconstruction. We must remember that in each and every case, we need to respond to an actual person with a world of personal experience. Following Levinas, I assert we are *duty-bound* to attend to the child's experience. I suggest we have an ethical duty to implement a compassionate approach which must *precede* our ongoing effort to create, reinterpret and enforce the law.

CHAPTER 3

Children's Identity: Constructing Memory through Law and Its Responsiveness to Children

> There were seventy of us in a forestry commando unit for Jewish prisoners of war in Nazi Germany ... the French uniform still protected us from Hitlerian violence. But the other men, called free, who had dealings with us or gave us work or orders or even a smile – and the children and women who passed by and sometimes raised their eyes – stripped us of our human skins. We were subhuman, a gang of apes. A small inner murmur. the strength and wretchedness of persecuted people, reminded us of our essence as thinking creatures, but we were no longer part of the world. Our comings and goings, our sorrow and laughter. Illnesses and distractions, the work of our hands and the anguish of our eyes, the letters we received from France and those accepted for our families – all that passed in parenthesis. We were beings entrapped in their species; despite their vocabulary, beings without language ... Social aggression shuts people away in a class, deprives them of expression and condemns them to being 'signifiers without a signified' and from there to violence and fighting. How can we deliver a message about our humanity which, from behind the bars of quotation marks, will come across as anything other than monkey talk?
>
> And then, about halfway through our long captivity, for a few short weeks, before the sentinels chased him away, a wandering dog entered our lives. One day he came to meet this rabble as we returned under guard from work. He survives in some wild patch in the region of the camp. But we called him Bobby, an exotic name, as one does with a cherished dog. He would appear at morning assembly and was waiting for us as we returned, jumping up and down and barking in delight. For him there was no doubt that we were men.
>
> This dog was the last Kantian in Nazi Germany, without the brain needed to universalize maxims and drives.
>
> LEVINAS 1997, 152–153

I Introduction

Society's unacknowledged conflict over its collective memory and the question of responsibility to the Other encourages politicizing empathy towards

 | DOI 10.1163/9789004223677_004

children. What we fail to recognize is how dynamic and conflictual the process of remembering and othering is. This chapter describes how professionals who fail to reflect on this conflict can also neglect to respond to individual suffering. I also argue that alienated doctrinal thinking cannot appreciate the value in of face-to-face dialogue with the individual when constructing legal norms. Thus it facilitates rationalizing politicized empathy and doing away with our sense of injustice. Dangerously, from my perspective, such doctrinal thinking can also be couched in rights rhetoric.

Two partially overlapping issues illustrate this chapter's thesis:

1. The protection of family lives for children from disadvantaged homes.
2. The public response to the past victimization of young offenders.

Drawing on the autobiographical opening vignette and on the discussion of Levinas's thought in the previous chapter I suggest here how law, through either perpetuating alienation from the Other or attempting to overcome it, is as an author of memory. I tie this suggestion to the challenge of psychological mindedness presented by Therapeutic Jurisprudence. I explain how law can be more than a rationalization of selective remembering and resulting politicized empathy, and how we can struggle more mindfully over the law's construction of collective memory. The chapter does not purport to offer a comprehensive discussion of the law in any one country, but draws rather on examples from different countries. I do not bring the examples to prove my thesis but to allow the reader the opportunity to be convinced by its feasibility.

II Alienation, Children's Experience and Doctrinal Thinking

One must concede that feelings can be irrational. On the other hand, though, rationality can degenerate into rationalization justifying the dehumanization of the Other. The child can also be the Other: the child offender, the illegal immigrant's child, or the enemy's child can be subject to othering. Legal intervention can also be traumatic to the child but the traumatizing, painful aspect of judicial decision making is often denied, ignored or underplayed (Cover 1998).

In the autobiographical vignette opening this chapter, Levinas hints that rationalization ensnares us. Despite being captive to doctrinal thinking, which excuses our attitudes and behavior, we delude ourselves that we are free, because we can reason. This is rationalization along the lines, of 'I think and can ethically justify my behavior towards the child. Therefore, I am acting ethically towards him'. As we have seen in the previous chapter, Levinas's thought highlights the potential weakness of human rights discourse. It clarifies its potential to degenerate into an alienated discourse justifying self-centeredness.

How do developments in international child law, primarily the consolidation and universal ratification of the Convention and the operation of the United Nations Committee on the Rights of the Child, relate to the risk of dehumanizing the child as Other?

To a large extent, international children's rights law may be no more than new universal ethics. The Committee on the Rights of the Child frightens no one. It interprets a document comprised mainly of principles, and one wonders what societies in ratifying states will make of the Convention and the Committee's observations. I suspect that if they rationalize present practices, they will make little of both.

Levinas draws on his experience to explain how the capacity to respond humanely does not demand the capacity to reason, generalize or universalize as an indispensable condition.

What he is telling us is that he regained something of the human dignity denied to him by his captors and the German civilians he met through the responsiveness of a dog.

I suggest, following our discussion in the last chapter, that to understand better children's world view, hopes and dreams, we must face children in all their subjectivity and uniqueness. Until then, we may find only peace or refuge in half-truths patched together to avoid disturbing the status quo or our professed commitment to the Convention's ethos (Weiner 1991).

A construction of childhood alienated from children's experience can degenerate into a refusal to admit available data incongruent occurrences. If, and to the extent that it is genuine false consciousness, it has a built in resistance to recognizing its own falsity (Nandy 2004). Drawing inspiration from Levinas, as interpreted in the previous chapter, we can envision a level of responsiveness to children's needs that leads to recognition of general and universal norms.

Returning to the vignette opening this chapter, what does Levinas mean when he writes 'This dog was the last Kantian in Nazi Germany, without the brain needed to universalize maxims and drives'?

For Kant, rationalist reasoning is the ultimate source of morality (Kant 2004). In pursuance to my discussion in the second chapter, I suggest that Levinas is not dismissing in these words the value of reason or the capacity to generalize or universalize. Rather, I believe the 'twist' in his self-contradictory, bitter, pseudo-recognition of the dog as the last Kantian does not stem from cynicism or disdain for Kant's vision of morality. Rather, it stems from a sad disillusionment with the influence Kant's vision on Pre-World War II Germany.

A general or universal norm need not be alienated from experience. The subjective can lead to the intersubjective, and the intersubjective can legitimately lead to constructing a general and universal human rights-children's rights norm. A children's rights doctrine can be responsive to children's experience. However, the aloofness of an intellectual frame of mind-drawing satisfaction from its own ability to philosophize and rationalize creates the risk of alienating both human rights advocates and scholars from children's experience.

III Self-Constructing Identity and Remembering as Dynamic Processes

We actively construct personal and group memory. Actively, because memory involves perpetual activity: it does not simply exist but is built and continuously altered. Thus, remembering is a dynamic process of reinterpretation (Ronen 2006).

On the personal level, if, say in psychotherapy, a violent adolescent recalls childhood abuse of which he was always partly conscious, his memory of who caused that abuse, the object of his anger and his own identity can radically change. By isolating him from society, a juvenile offender who is institutionalized and later imprisoned becomes fairly insignificant as a prospective agent for social change. If, however, he identifies his past abuse as a result of systemic injustice, he may use his anger to fight for social change and challenge that injustice. Thus, a formative life experience such as psychotherapy can provide a powerful directedness to the dynamic process of reinterpretation of personal history. This process of reinterpretation has been described as rebiography (Rotenberg 1987; Maruna 2001, 165–168).

Let me exemplify my point: Israeli law differentiates between parents and other caretakers in relation to mandatory reporting of offenses against children. It is the duty of all individuals to report the suspicion of abuse by a parent or legal guardian either to a child protection officer or to the police. In contrast if an offense against a child is committed by staff at an institution in which a child was placed for his own good, one is not duty-bound to report the offense. Only if severe injury or a sex offense has been committed is there a duty to report the offense, and then only by the staff of the institution, who may be fired the next day as a result of fulfilling a statutory duty. Now let us imagine a violent, turbulent seventeen- years old adolescent, we shall call him Tom, who was institutionalized between the ages of ten and twelve because of parental neglect. Tom gets involved in fights with his peers and even slapped his teacher once when he humiliated him in front of the class. Everyone around him sees Tom as an angry and violent adolescent. Tom initially blames mainly himself for his ongoing physical abuse by institutional staff and bullying by his peers at the institution, though this abuse brought about a change in his behavior patterns and aggravated his anger and aggression. Tom may discover through psychotherapy the responsibility for his suffering including the violence he experienced, lies not only with the perpetrators and institutional staff who were silent bystanders. He may learn it lies also with legislators, policy makers and child advocates who knowingly let his voice to be silenced by backing a system of selective mandatory reporting, trusting the system where biological kin are no longer trusted.

He may also come to see that his sense of humiliation and powerlessness at his removal from home because of neglect, only to fall prey to institutional abuse, and his deep bitterness at never being visited by the child protection officer who took him from his home, are a symptom of child and family policy. He may question the skewed distribution of funds by Israeli child welfare, which channels most of its funds to institutions whose quality of care varies considerably and fails to allocate social rights to children within their families and communities, rights, which might have helped avoid his out of home placement.

It is not inconceivable that sooner or later Tom may play an important role in advocacy for the reform of child protection law. He may do this through recourse to his own valuable personal experience. Thus, he may push for the equalization of mandatory reporting between abuse at home and in institutions, for allocation of social rights for children within their families and communities and for mandatory periodic visits by child protection workers to children in institutions and for the accountability of these workers to the children. In such a case, the child has no memory in the sense of an intact picture to be retrieved. Rather his mind contains elements of past and present that are linked and differentiated in a very individual and unique way (Minow 1998, 120). However, Tom's personal testimony has unique power in the public discourse, and his reported experience is commonly perceived as 'the' truth or at least his truth.

Constructing memory through psychotherapy involves a rather slow process of reinterpretation. At the societal level, precedential case law and new legislation, two mechanisms of the legal system, both express and facilitate reinterpreting memory (Minow 1998, 120). These mechanisms are fast routes in bringing about reinterpretation of collective memory and have a large-scale effect. They are ultimately mobilized by individuals, both laypersons who are social activists and professionals such as judges academic scholars and child advocates, whose identities and direction in life are dynamically self-constructed and influenced by formative events such as parenthood, psychotherapy, close friendships or mentoring. Remembering then, is a politically potent tool (Minow 1998, 119), though it is not necessarily utilized to promote social change, as the next example demonstrates.

History is a projection in the sense that individuals in positions of influence can project onto it the meaning of their choice, so that these projections become objective 'history', an account of the 'the facts', 'what really happened'. Thus, one can read meanings into history that relate to perceived personal and national needs and aspirations.

Let us now imagine seventeen-year-old Tom as an army draftee. He endures great physical and emotional challenges during his training, while being constantly reminded of his country's heroic national heritage, which is presented to him as part of his identity. The way the challenges are packaged, may thus affect the recruit's evolving, self-constructed national identity. It may change his memory of who he is, and radically change the source of his strength. He may learn to see his heroic national past as a key source of strength and inspiration. In a democratic regime, the rhetoric Tom is exposed to as part of his training naturally and typically mirrors to an extent collective memory as portrayed in public discourse. The public discourse on a country's national past – whether concerning images of reconciliation or conflict – can influence the lessons individual learn from both their own and their national history. Tom's case as a recruit only exemplifies a widespread phenomenon: we not only shape public discourse, we are shaped by it too.

IV Authoring Memory through Law and the Challenge of Psychological Mindedness

Regarding law and collective memory, law as culture, as a set of meanings, is loaded with selective memories and understandings based on those memories. By engaging these memories and understandings, the law defines society's rights holders. When conflict occurs in which memory is involved, the struggle is often between clashing ideologies or differing worldviews (Hom and Yamamoto 2000). One such struggle concerns how the law should respond to an offending, victimizing youth who himself has been exposed to abuse.

We find growing recognition in the literature that professionals should able to contain such ambiguities and that law mirroring this difficulty should not enslave helping professionals to its agenda of reconstructing reality in terms of binary divisions between innocence and culpability (Keddell 2011; King and Trowell 1995, 108–109).

Western legal culture is a culture of critique, which often does not allow the Other the benefit of the doubt and sanctifies skepticism (Wexler 2000; Orange 2011). Lawyers and their clients are often relegated to a gladiatorial, psychologically-blind style of law that often wreaked emotional damage upon all those involved with or touched by the legal process (Daicoff 2000). This section contends that psychological mindedness can gradually liberate law, jurists and helping professionals from some of the legal culture's shackling of our thinking and behavior. I use the term 'psychological mindedness' as an umbrella term to denote the capacity to reflect on ourselves, the Other, and the relationship between the Self and the Other. The term implies a curiosity about what moves people emotionally and why we behave as we do. It also concerns our ability to see the past in the present and to form links between current issues and past events (Hall 1992).

Thus, psychological mindedness prods us to examine critically dominant, official narratives, the official links between past and present, through the official construction of memory implicit in both case law and legislation. We are encouraged in this by our recognition that the shackles have loosened even before we begin. Jurists' current disillusionment with a legal culture of rivalry and belligerence may be slowly transforming the legal system into a more humane, healing and psychologically sophisticated agent in people's lives (Perlin, 2000; Daicoff 2000, 490). On the whole, a more psychologically healing approach advocated by the Therapeutic Jurisprudence Movement is gaining momentum (Perlin, 2000; Daicoff 2000, 490). Given that this is so, we may hope for a greater commitment to examining critically the tie between law's construction of memory and its responsiveness to children. Law is not only constrained by history and memory. It uses them as tools for legal reasoning. It may be seen as natural for a child advocate to choose whichever elements of the child's history he believes support his case. Though unsettling for some to contemplate, judges do much the same thing in their construction of the past. Their choice of words in describing the past is reconstructive.

Let us imagine a child consistently scapegoated by his father and stepmother who becomes a 'throwaway' – 'runaway' street child. Critically. A child protection worker alarmed at his association with offenders on the street is confident that recommending the court to sentence him to an institution mixing adolescent offenders and adolescents at risk is a reasonable course of action. She does this, though she failed to meet him in person because he refused to come. She sees nothing wrong with her failure to reveal the child's past victimization as she is overworked and diligent in her work. Because the child protection officer chooses not to explore past victimization, which may repeat itself, this adolescent at risk is not presented to the court as an abused, victimized child, but as a potential offender, a threat to the moral fibre of society, leaving the court ignorant of his victimization and affecting his sentence and his future. The judge may thus choose to adopt unquestioningly this characterization of the adolescent offered by the child protection officer. In choosing not to doubt this characterization the judge reconstructs this adolescent's history in collective memory through his judgment, a pronouncement of official truth.

Following Walant (1995), I would like us to consider the idea that there is always abuse which is normative within our culture.

Keeping this idea in mind, let us critically explore the official reading of the adolescent's history. Who is the greater moral threat to society – are we allowed to contemplate that it is not the confused adolescent but rather a helping professional who may through smugness and indifference becomes an accomplice of unresponsive parents? Or expressed in more general terms, is a child who is humiliated because of the color of his skin, his circumcision, or his ethnicity, who explodes emotionally at an emotionally distant teacher indifferent to bullying, exposed to normative abuse by an oppressive system or simply 'out of line'? How does and how should legal rhetoric relate to this type of painful adolescent memory of the school system?

Law's rejection of the child's counter-narrative through pathologizing its author (Ronen 1998, 263) or its willingness to integrate part of that narrative into the mainstream discourse, covertly takes place through court decisions. Occasionally, decisions do not mirror present public responsiveness to children, but frame future responsiveness by acknowledging unmet needs. It is not possible for courts to decide what norms to apply without choosing which facts to include in a legal decision and what meaning to award them. The common law fiction that judges relying solely on case law only declare law and never create it is founded on a covert and perpetual reinterpretation of the past: that interpreting legal precedents is the arena of legal controversy since different jurists reach conflicting conclusions concerning applicable norms based on the same case law. Indeed, each jurist has his own narrative, and what is constructed as legal history and compelling precedent is unavoidably a by-product of active reinterpretation of collective memory.

In light of my discussion in the previous chapter, I suggest that the Brown Case (1954) is importantly a child advocacy case deeply tied to the legal reconstruction of African American identity – The social group most harmfully humiliated by segregation is children.

Yet, as explained in the previous chapter, the humiliation caused by segregation did not start in 1954, when a politically conscious court decided to respond to it promoting equality for African-Americans. The court through dramatically re- interpreting the Fourteenth Amendment to the American Constitution, which had been the cornerstone for decisions affirming racial segregation, reconstructed historical memory. Though, the court in the Brown case found support in social science evidence, it would be naïve to conclude that what had delayed such a decision for decades was the lack of such evidence (Mody 2004; Siegel 2004). The court made a conscious decision to respond to African-American experience and to a sense of injustice, through reinterpreting the meaning of racial equality in American Constitutional Law. Thus, through radical reconstructing memory, it challenged a false consciousness of fairness and decency towards African-Americans, one that is alienated from the experience of many of them. Unsurprisingly, the decision attracted violent resistance from those committed to the status quo it sought to change. Sadly it achieved less than its authors may have hope for (Sitbon 2008; Love 2004). A psychologically conscious court became an uninvited and disputed author-inventor of national memory. This form of legal activism is in itself worthy of recognition in my eyes.

V Struggling over Memory

Often when trying to bring about social change by revealing children's experience, we, in fact, challenge memory. Conceptualizing racial segregation as discrimination, corporal punishment as child abuse, paternalistic child welfare practices as the silencing of children, or advertising sexualizing children as child abuse are all examples of challenging memory.

These challenges may be fought off as contradictory to common sense by those opposed to recognizing suffering and to law's responsiveness to it through recognizing new rights (Rogers 1989, 285).

Returning to the Brown Case, its aftermath is perhaps the prime example of such a struggle and of active turbulent resistance to a judicial attempt to challenge the meaning of responsiveness to the Other. This resistance cannot erase the decision's impact on collective memory.

One could compare the opposition to law's responsiveness to the child as Other to the opposition women and slaves faced when demanding human rights being perceived by society as the property of white men. Similarly, the notion that gladiatorial combat is not a sport or that all children benefit from the right to schooling or from the right not to work even if work allows them to help their families, was commonly perceived as unacceptable and weird. Thus, what may seem common sense at one time can, at another times, be regarded as absurd, cruel or unjust. Moreover, it is not easy to perceive the development of collective memory in real time as it occurs. Tomorrow's heroes are liable to become today's targets of abuse and ridicule.

Children are a vulnerable group and psychological defenses have been used for centuries to deny cruelty and abuse towards children. It is useful to recall that at times, child abuse was widespread and socially acceptable. Greek philosophers supported both sexually abusive behaviors towards adolescents and slavery. These philosophers were not fundamentally evil. Simply, their moral sensitivity, in the Levinasian sense, was not deep enough to encompass disempowered groups such as children and slaves, and the collective memory had no space to admit their suffering (Nandy 1990, 32–33, 47–50).

On the one hand, we purposefully revise our collective memory through legal discourse. On the other hand, though, for good examples of collective memory revision, we must step outside the legal sphere. In the past century, Mahatma Gandhi's struggle against indentured labor and segregation of untouchables and Martin Luther King's struggle against segregation are examples of threatening attempts to change collective memory, attempts, which may have contributed to the motivation to murder them. Their starting point was their own sense of self-worth, which allowed them to transform their world view and memories of their own past without feeling insecure, self-worth, which the Convention's regime now aims to promote universally (Rogers 1989, Erikson 1970).

We should venture to ask whether we allow ourselves to respond empathically to the difficulties of a neglecting and abused mother or to the past abuse of a violent adolescent? These are politically loaded questions, which challenge the present allocation of power between the mother and the child protection system or between an offending adolescent and the juvenile justice system.

Case law contains many examples of empathy and antipathy towards different individuals. Reading the purported 'facts' of a case often leads subconsciously to an empathic stance toward the 'suffering parent' or 'humiliated child' or conversely, to indignant disgust or rejection of the 'abusive parent' or 'disturbed child'. The choice of who receives our empathy is a political choice in the sense that it allocates power to those we judge worthy of empathy. Their narrative becomes the official, dominant, narrative and part of the collective memory, and the narrative of the excluded is likely to be forgotten. We must also recall that legislators, judges and policy makers often caution themselves against yielding to empathy, and dichotomize between reason and emotion (Minow 1990, 1665–1699). The result is a tendency to empathize only with what they remember as painful or unjust and having decided which norms should apply retroactively, rationalize their politicized choices as stemming from legal theory. Reflective practice (Kinsella 2010; Schon 1983) can help to democratize the politics of empathy towards children. It can do this both by making decision makers more sharply aware of their accountability for their choices and by making empathic choices open to public analysis. Once the choices are made, we should suspend moral judgment to allow ourselves to understand the full personal meaning of the Other's experience and articulate an empathic narrative.

As noted earlier, one issue in child law that illustrates this chapter's thesis is the issue of protecting the family life of children from disadvantaged homes.

VI Protecting the Family Lives of Children from Disadvantaged Homes

A Language of Comprehensive Protection from All Harm

We often define a child in need of state protection as any child who may suffer emotional or physical harm. We often formulate the aim of child protection law as preventing all such harm to the child, whether by action or inaction (Sutherland 1999, 293; Fortin 1998, 368–371; Van Bueren 1998, 88; Kilkelly 1999, 160; Meriwether 1986, 149–150). On the whole, legal systems do not adopt a narrow definition of child abuse with a conclusive list of factual situations of abuse. The given rationale is often that an open-ended definition of abuse enables responsiveness to different types of abuse (Fortin 1998, 368–371; Lyon and De Cruz 1993, 5; Sutherland 1999, 292–293; Sharon 1998, 323, 349–350; Reifen 1978, 215). Different legal clauses may refer to different instances of abuse and neglect, but typically most do not explicitly mention the behavior of the child's parents or the behavior of those responsible for her. Child protection law is predominantly civil law. Therefore, strictly speaking, formally, parents are not accused and not punished through child protection law. Ostensibly, It is not their blameworthiness, which determines the outcome of the proceedings but rather the child's well-being.

Van Bueren (1998, 88) explains the non-definition of abuse and neglect in international law aims to prevent basing definitions of abuse and neglect on ethnocentric or arbitrary assumptions.

Thus, when observing child law, whether as laypersons exposed to the media, as legislators, or as jurists, we are often gently guided through the wording of the statutes and case law. We remain with the memory that the state offers the child comprehensive protection from all abuse and neglect and does not target parents as prime subjects for reprisal.

How State Action to Protect Children Can Miss Their Needs

Laws often assume implicitly the primary risk to children stems from those directly responsible for them, and that it is from these individuals children should be chiefly protected by the law. Child protection thus becomes the focal point of child welfare practices for social workers and other child welfare professionals (Guggenheim 2000, 1749–1750; Cooper, Baistow, Hetherington, Pitts and Spriggs 1995; Brooks and Ronen 2006).

In contrast to the comprehensive definition of the child who needs state protection, in practice, we may find that child welfare consistently excludes the larger, more pressing issues that affect children's well-being. Child welfare as a Western social construct gives a twisted, narrow, picture. A narrow picture of child welfare policy chiefly focuses on children harmed by their own families, and the apparatus and policies of state action aim to find and protect such children. However, is the problem of children harmed by their parents the most pressing issue in child welfare? Is it the key to protecting children?

Strategies that broaden the lens of problems facing children and maximize the chance of children being raised by their own willing families are hardly ever used. Children are denied basic necessities. Not surprisingly, children from socially marginalized groups are liable to suffer most from this approach. In both the legal and public discourse, the tie between social exclusion and injustice and identification as at risk has not been made (Guggenheim 2000, 1749–1750). The law can protect children based on proof of need. However, it runs the risk of seeing parents as solely responsible for responding to the child's needs. Thus, it may become preoccupied with evidential issues of parental wrongdoing to justify intervention (Featherstone, White and Morris 2014; Cooper, Baistow, Hetherington, Pitts and Spriggs 1995) neglecting the social reality underlying the child's unmet needs. Evidential preoccupation is neither inevitable nor derived from the law's fundamental nature (Madden and Wayne 2003). However, it is easy to fall into a formalistic, soulless preoccupation with procedure and evidence. Thus, achieving recognition of the child's authentic needs as a whole person tied to family and community still challenges countries committed to the Convention's rights regime.

To summarize, in the collective memory, an open-ended definition of abuse, coupled with interventions solely focused on protecting the child from his family, creates a distorted picture of childhood, the hazards children face, and the state protection offered. The implications of this distortion can be diverse and far reaching.

Politics of Unrecognition and the Invisibility of Children's Experiences

Once harm to the child is identified, the child's interests are often paramount, and he may receive a remedy under child law, despite infringement of the interests of others, such as biological kin, foster parents or adoptive parents.

As a result of the struggle between children's rights proponents and the proponents of family autonomy and parental rights, the present state of child protection law in the West signifies, on the whole, clear progress for the child's interests in the post-World War II era. State protection from harm for children has widened in scope and now mandates greater intervention into family life, despite infringement of what used to be perceived in the past as parental rights (e.g. Gilat 2015).

Seeing this, one might be tempted to argue that comprehensive paramountcy of children's interests under law has been achieved. Moreover, commitment to the child's interests in specific situations of proven harm and compassionate rhetoric in case law, public inquiries and parliamentary debates, may naturally lead us to assume that this commitment reflects comprehensive state responsibility for the child. However, in taking this view, we are tempted to forget what is probably the most important insight in Goldstein, Solnit and Freud's trilogy on the best interests of the child. This insight, which has been incorporated into case law in different jurisdictions, proposes that state action to protect the child is always only the least detrimental alternative. Therefore, it is not the equivalent of paramountcy of children's interests under law. The relationship between adoption, foster care and poverty exemplifies this. In an ideal society, adoption would be an accepted but rare alternative for children whose parents cannot take care of them or choose not to. An ideal society would radically decrease its need for adoption by combating poverty and its dangers to children (Roberts 1999; Cahn 1999). To paraphrase Gary Melton, the question now is whether a system that developed from intrusion into the lives of the poor can be reconstituted to provide services that can nurture the quality of the lives of all children (Melton 1994, 38). This question assumes greater force when socially regressive child and family policies lead to poverty in a large proportion of families. When the poor are no longer a very small minority, exclusive emphasis on intrusive intervention in family life in the name of children's rights leads to a 'democratic deficit' (Mundlac 2003): When a large segment of the population suffers from the policies that target it and becomes powerless through the politics of unrecognition, one cannot but conclude that democracy in its deeper more pervasive meaning has been compromised. The present international rights regime has not created effective mechanisms for combating the unrecognition of children's sense of belonging to a family and community and their suffering when subjected to outdated noninterventionist social policies built on false assumptions of equal opportunities (Novoa 1999, 43). Thus, the experiences of these children become invisible in the collective memory. Following our discussion in the previous chapter we can safely suggest the following: Levinas would see it as only natural that his discussion of his invisible humanness – buried under a constructed memory of the Jew – can be utilized to understand why the experience of children from disadvantaged homes becomes invisible despite recourse to doctrinal rights discourse. In both cases, the human intellect is harnessed while neglecting to come to terms with the subjective, personal assault on our senses: Thus, in both cases experience disappears.

If we take the United States as an example, we find that not only is a disproportionate number of foster care children from minority cultures, but they are also overwhelmingly poor (Roberts 1999; Cahn 1999). These demographics hold true for many other societies, including Israel. In practice, our societies generally respect the privacy and autonomy of middle-class families, but we accede to coercive intervention and intrusion in low-income or otherwise excluded disempowered families, by convincing ourselves that such interventions are unavoidable from a child-centered perspective (Brooks and Ronen 2006; Ronen and Ben Harush 2005; Ronen 2005). We discount and devalue the cultural backgrounds and solid parenting skills of many such disempowered parents. In trying to protect children, we often neglect their parents' needs and interests and their communities' cooperative values, and thus mainstream society evades the responsibility for the flawed development of children from these families. It is less painful psychologically to point an accusing finger at dysfunctional parents then to face our responsibility for the systemic causes for malfunctioning (Brooks and Ronen 2006).

The American child welfare system has been castigated as a coercive system that thrives on punishment and blame of the poor. The othering of poor families in the US context, particularly when they are of color, makes it easy for the dominant culture to devalue them: to view them as dysfunctional and not families at all. Annette Appell, a proponent of openness in adoption, has criticized the 'growth industry' that has arisen from the state's 'protective' involvement with poor families and families of color and the state's punitive treatment, particularly of the mothers of these families. These mothers are outside norms and myths of white, middle-class mothering in several ways, including the simple fact that they are poor, but also because they depend on informal kinship and community networks for child care. Similar observations have been made concerning the Israeli context (Brooks and Ronen 2006; Ronen and Ben Harush 2005).

Many of the same families whose 'cultures' are marginalized and misunderstood by the child welfare system are also affected by domestic violence. The above discussion thus also applies with equal force to cases of domestic violence. The othering of those exposed to violence makes it easier for us to condemn them for their choices and to fail to appreciate the complexities of their situations.

Fostering Children's Self-Actualization While Protecting Them

The ethos of liberal individualism does not foster state responsibility for hunger, homelessness, violent educational environment, inadequate healthcare, or nonexistent counseling services for children whose working parents are at times physically absent and emotionally spent (Cover 1998, 239–248). Children exposed to such hazards are often ignorant and apathetic regarding civil liberties such as freedom of expression freedom of conscience or freedom of education. They have little chance of becoming the autonomous adults who widely exercise these liberties, as liberal theory imagines they do. Often, such individuals even if they are aware of their liberties, perceive them as irrelevant to their struggles and worries, which, to a degree, makes sense.

The liberal individualist ethos has led me and other to use an economic rationale for allocating social rights under child protection law. This approach, though not blameworthy if it achieves recognition of children's social rights, nevertheless, highlights the public blindness to an instrumental approach to children's needs. If a society genuinely respects children, it will invest in their social rights – not because it is cheaper than investing in long-term institutionalization. It will do so, because it recognizes that their rights to identity and to family life stem from their fundamental human dignity as interdependent human beings as explained in Chapter 1. There is no need to turn to an economic rationale for justifying social rights. Children, we know, can develop complex identifications, which despite abuse or neglect by the family and community, often remain important to them. An atomistic or individualistic ethos does not foster authentic self- actualization in children nor recognize the importance of family and community ties to forming identity (see e.g. Zafran 2010).

We must also remember that protecting the child's identity and autonomy is different from protecting the same in adults. To value a child's evolving capacities and partial autonomy is to respect her conceptions of others, even though she does not start with plans or conceptions (Appiah 1994, 158). Here, liberal individualism comes to our aid.

There is a danger, however, that liberal, individualistic rights discourse might aid reconstructing the social problem of harm to children as a question of private disputes between individuals. According to this reconstruction, the sole role of the state would be the advocacy of the child opposite those who are intimately responsible for her well-being.

Furthermore, the absolute quality of individualistic 'rights talk' heightens social conflict and inhibits dialogue possibly leading toward consensus or at least the discovery of a common ground. Moreover, it contributes to the othering of vulnerable populations, which fosters a climate that systematically disadvantages caretakers and is alienated from society's so called 'losers' (Brooks and Ronen 2006).

In individualistic rights discourse, the traditional image of the state as one corner of a triangle and the parents and their children as the other two corners (an image of rivalry and competition) is one expression of this reconstruction. The state and parents may indeed compete sometimes and rival each other in the struggle to determine what is best for the child and to uphold the child's interests. However, for children to develop their potential, the state should serve primarily as one of many resources open to the child and his family. I hope the distortion of children's needs implicit in the traditional liberal individualistic ethos is gaining greater recognition. Less emphasis on rigid unconstrained individualism and more emphasis on preserving relationships, connectedness and identity within a family and community in developing children's rights may indicate such recognition as explained in Chapter 1.

The preceding arguments may lead to important questions: For example, do we empathically understand the narrative of a poor and neglectful mother who receives taxpayers' support? From a genuinely child-centered perspective, can we morally afford not to offer her help? Is the price that children pay for the liberal individualistic ethos behind the legal rhetoric acceptable in as much as it is blind to social injustice and the lack of opportunities for the excluded poor children? Is children's rights discourse naturally responsive to their experience?

How Can Children's Counter-Narratives Reconstruct Children's Rights Discourse?

The above discussion leading to its concluding questions highlights the pitfalls of misusing the terminology of individual rights to frame child and family policy ignoring children's counter-narratives. However, international law, primarily in the form of the Convention, is an articulation of children's rights that demonstrates the potential for a rights-based framework to reflect an ethos of interdependence rather than rigid individualism. As explained in the opening chapter, the Convention serves as a solid foundation on which to construct a children's rights regime based on interdependence, affirming the reciprocal attachments of the child and her family and community (for a noteworthy critique of the Convention's ethos, sharing the concern with attention to children's counter-narratives see Barnes 2013).

My criticism of liberal individualism that often underlies children's rights discourse does not negate the value of the discourse. It highlights the danger of its distortion and misuse. Fully enabling and facilitating children's participation in decisions that affect them is indispensable if we are to achieve the genuine state responsibility for child protection envisaged here.

We have seen how alienated doctrinal thinking, which does not appreciate the value of face-to-face dialogue with the individual when constructing legal norms, perpetuates rationalizing politicized empathy and abrogating our sense of injustice. Dangerously, such thinking can also be couched in rights rhetoric.

A language of needs implies an assessment of needs, but may lead to children's objectification. The common conception of professionalism in child protection, calls for children's needs assessment to be based on objectifiable factors. However, this may serve to disempower children, who may have difficulty expressing anger and frustration towards professionals who they feel have treated them unjustly. Some professionals view children in need of protection simply as children with problems that must be assessed in order to identify needs objectively, disregard children's unique strengths and ignore their ability to overcome adversity. The individual child with no right to participate in defining her own abuse and neglect and what she believes can protect her against them under the law cannot effectively challenge those professionals. Only by acknowledging children's strengths in adversity can we genuinely respect the child's human dignity as an individual capable of self-actualization (Featherstone, White and Morris 2014).

Enabling and facilitating children's participation acknowledging their evolving capacities and strengths will bring counter-narratives to the forefront. Thus, we can reveal, how our understanding of the injustices and suffering children endure is limited.

How Can We Humanize Young Offenders?

The murder of James Bulger in 1993 was a horrendous event in which not only was a child horribly murdered, but his parents and everyone who knew and cared for him suffered indescribable trauma. It was this trauma, as will now be demonstrated, the law justifiably chose to relate. And it was for this reason that only twenty minutes of the seventeen-day trial were devoted to the mental state of the two accused minors. I shall not dwell here at length on the possible victimization of these child offenders through legal proceedings blind to their special needs. This issue was widely discussed by both the courts and in the literature (e.g. Buckley 2002). The trial and later setting of tariff by the Home Secretary vulnerable to influence by public opinion were held by the European Court of Human Rights to be in violation of the European Convention for the Protection of Human Rights and Fundamental Freedoms. More specifically the court held the two children could not participate effectively in the public and highly publicized proceedings and were, in consequence, denied a fair hearing (Case of T.V.U.K. 1999, Case of V.V.U.K. 1999).

Judge Morland, presiding over the case, described the killing as a cunning and wicked act of unparalleled evil and brutality (R. v. Secretary of State 1998). He continued by elegantly blocking the view to what might have been perceived as mitigating factors in the public's image of the boys: "It is not for me to pass judgment on their upbringing, but I suspect exposure to violent video games may in part be an explanation" (R. v. Secretary of State 1998). Nowhere is there any mention of the social and economic causes of the crime (see also Smith 1995; Jackson 1995; Freeman 1997, 244).

The judge never explained why the court should not pass judgment on the children's upbringing, even though in this statement, he was indeed passing judgment. Note, however, the question of responsibility for the children's upbringing was never explored. Implicitly, the boys' parents were responsible for their children's upbringing, but out of respect for family privacy and the parents' dignity, the court refrained from tarring them with a more explicit moral accusation. Shifting the focus to violent video games served to reposition the question of responsibility in an impersonal, asocial sphere. Dismissed by the court, it was left to post-trial academic research to clarify the children's family and social background.

How did the court demonization of the two compare with other constructions affecting the collective British memory? Can we envision an alternative to demonization at one pole and complete innocence at the other when faced with such a terrible act? The then British Prime Minster, John Major, called for greater condemnation and less understanding. The politicization of empathy in this case involving professional politicians created an invisible barrier between the public and the murdering children.

The minister of state for probation services at the time lambasted the church for spending its time discussing social issues and leaving the politicians to debate right and wrong – implying that social issues do not involve questions of right and wrong (Collett 1993).

I want to suggest the important question here is who were the two boys? – is there anything for us to know or understand – or were they just two evil boys?

The psychiatrists who examined the two boys declared them free of mental illness or depression, although there was plenty of evidence hinting that these were very unhappy, emotionally disturbed boys who were consequently problematic in various ways. Jon's background seems chronically insecure as he gets shunted back and forth between parents who suffer from periodic depression, cannot cope consistently, nor decide whether to live together or apart. At the age of seven, a trainee psychologist identifies him as unable to cope with the pressures on him. Bobby came from a history of neglect and violence. Bobby's mother was herself an abused and unloved child, marries an abusive violent man with whom she has six children. Once Bobby's father leaves, she starts drinking heavily. Bullying brothers take over disciplining Bobby. Both boys stole, bullied other children, underachieved scholastically and were often truant. Neither received significant attention of helping professionals prior to the murder. Both received it in secure accommodation and radically changed their behavior. Bobbie moved from habitual truant to college student (Jefferson 1996).

The politicians' statements imply that social issues do not involve questions of right and wrong. They also imply that if the child murderers had been taught to understand the meaning of 'wrong' and condemned for their misdeeds in the past, the murder would never have happened. Furthermore, they imply that society's efforts to understand the causes of crime undermine its efforts to prevent it. Here we should note the contrasting approach of the United Nations Guidelines for the Prevention of Juvenile Delinquency. The guidelines chiefly discuss the systemic social and economic factors that can ensure psychological well-being and advocate a proactive, preventive approach (Cappelaere 1995).

The premises of both the judge's and the politicians' rhetoric are unfounded. There is no basis for believing the boys were born evil, as Judge Morland intimated when writing of a wicked act of unparallel evil and brutality while almost totally ignoring their background. Neither is there a basis for thinking that had the boys understood the wrongness of their act and experienced condemnation for it in the past, they could have avoided the murder by themselves nor that attempting to understand the etiology of the terrible crime would undermine future efforts at crime prevention.

The sentence handed down and the politician's pronouncements all worked to the same end, to absolve Society and State from the moral responsibility for social problems.

Children who murder are a social problem and may reflect severe social neglect. However, I suggest we are all prone to anxiety at our vulnerability to such horrific behaviors and at the fragility of decency and humaneness in alienated social worlds where the claim that 'anything goes' is popular. I assert that this anxiety is exasperated by the perceived threat of postmodernism and Communitarianism, in as much as they are equated with justification of an a-moral social sphere. We are tempted to react to such anxiety by intolerance to ambiguity and uncertainty and scapegoating of an evil Other. Thus, a case like this becomes an excellent bludgeon to attack those who argue the state's responsibility for social ills. The Bulger murder was a horrific and twisted cry for attention and help. Key players in the British establishment used it to promote an agenda of social alienation. Can society afford to ignore the subjective meaning of the children's terrible act from their perspective? Can we deny our responsibility for the preconditions which must be tackled if we hope to lessen such horrors in the future? There is wide recognition in the literature that Society failed the children who murdered James Bulger (Downing 1994). We should translate such recognition into consolidation of social rights to services for children and their families such as tutoring, psychotherapy, school counseling and day care, services, which have a preventive effect and are called for by the Convention and the Ryadh Guidelines (Katz 2010; Cappelaere 1995).

The collective memory of these murders, the causes of the offenders' behavior, and the extent to which the state was responsive to the offenders' psychological and educational needs before the crime, is relevant for preventing child and adolescent violence and promoting individual and social well-being.

Through either the mindful or unmindful construction of the official and thus dominant narrative and the neglect of the children's counter-narratives, the judge in the Bulger case not only applied his own personal vision of human motivation, but justified a particular social philosophy through his pronouncement on reality. Under different circumstances, this philosophy would have seemed repugnant since it facilitated and excused state irresponsibility for children's twisted development. The two children, who came from disadvantaged homes and were undoubtedly harmed not only by unique family circumstances, but also by systemic and societal neglect, were not faced as human beings by either politicians or judges. Justifiably, they were held accountable for their terrible crime, but paradoxically, the terrible cruelty of the crime may have motivated the rationalization of a position of state non- accountability for the causes of child and juvenile delinquency.

Empathy in this case was blatantly politicized, humanizing professionalism-one that sees the offending children as suffering human beings and not objects of treatment, worthy of dignity (Featherstone, White, and Morris 2014) – was missing from public and legal discourse at the time of the trial.

Indeed, commenting about the case in ways that could have been construed as understanding the boys, could have deeply offended public sentiment. Nevertheless, humanizing the offenders despite their deeply shaking crime, and trying publicly to understand the causes of the murder might have served a person-centered agenda for child and family policy and could well have prevented future killings.

VII Conclusion

I opened this chapter with an autobiographical vignette describing how Emmanuel Levinas, its author, regained something of his human dignity denied to him by humans, through the responsiveness of a dog.

The vignette's author though disillusioned with a morality founded on intellect alone does not despair of the law's capacity to respond to human suffering.

Law is not inherently unresponsive to vulnerability and thus one should not despair of the prospect of its responsiveness to the experience of children, a social group characterized by vulnerability.

Indeed, individuals such as psychotherapists, novelists, judges, legislators and legal scholars who are able to influence our personal and collective memory can project the meanings of their choice onto our collective and personal pasts. Such projections may even become part of an ostensibly objective 'history', part of 'the facts', part of 'the true account of events'.

As legal history unfurls, narratives of childhood and parenthood are written and rewritten mainly because our understanding of our own childhood and the childhood of others changes as our personal memory is perpetually reconstructed.

This process does not have to be arbitrary, unconscious or unmindful.

Psychological mindedness can gradually liberate law, jurists and helping professionals from some of the legal culture's shackling of our thinking and behavior. Irrational reductionist skepticism can give way to a more balanced approach which is ready to risk trusting children and their families despite personal and familial deviance and malfunctioning.

Having pointed out the pitfalls of misusing the terminology of individual rights to frame child and family policy, we saw above the Convention provides a solid foundation upon which to set up a regime based on interdependence. What this means specifically is that the children's rights principles laid out in the Convention affirm the reciprocal attachments of the child and his family and community.

The arguments regarding adolescent offenders with which this chapter concludes exemplify the complexity and delicacy of constructing collective memory. Individuals who are harmed not only by familial abuse and neglect, but also by systemic and societal neglect often commit the most disturbing offenses. These individuals have to be faced as human beings despite the strong temptation to demonize them.

Revealing the politicization of empathy and committing ourselves to psychological mindedness may enable us to see a richer picture of the past.

Our memory of the past will frame our future, and we can offer our children a more responsive and humane world in which to grow to the degree that we allow ourselves to remember the inhumanity in our past.

CHAPTER 4

The Child's Right to Be Oneself

I Introduction

In Chapter 1, I explained that the state should have a positive duty to safeguard the child's right to identity as a right to protection of ties that are meaningful to the child. I suggested that these are primarily ties to the human world, but they can also be ties to an animal, to an inanimate object, or to a geographic place. I further suggested that through the proposed right to identity – currently not protected through either international or national laws – children's rights regimes should ideally be responsive to two complementing needs: the need to be|| and the need to become. In this chapter, in which my attention is dedicated solely to the conceptual level, I return to explore the child's need to be himself.

II Neglect of the Need 'to Be' and a Preoccupation with Material Progress

As explained in Chapter 1, the notion of individualized identity draws support from an ideal of authenticity, in the sense of being true to oneself and to one's particular way of being. Alongside the child's need to be different from others, there is the child's need to simply be. Advocates of children's rights often neglected the need to be. Protecting what the child sees as emotionally belonging to him may allow developing and enriching his moral and spiritual stature.

I suggest that the typical neglect of the child's need to be himself is associated with western culture's preoccupation with material progress. Because western culture is proud of its scientific achievements, economic progress, and ever-increasing knowledge acquisition, it values educated people more than non-educated people (Heneman 2006, 78–80). The roots of this western preoccupation with progress can be found in the Romans' disdain and ridicule of the Jewish Sabbath, on which work is prohibited (Heschel 1951). This emphasis on progress prompts to ask: Is there value to our lives if we do not produce, progress, build or create? – Do we have to be useful all the time? India's traditional approach to these questions is illustrative of a regime that values the mindset of simply being, The polar extreme of western culture's preoccupation with material progress. Within India, there are still cultural communities and

 DOI 10.1163/9789004223677_005

practices that have led to it being described as a world that is all Sabbath, a world in which material progress is not highly valued and is sometimes totally abandoned in favor of spiritual progress through well-trodden paths within traditional cultures (Heneman 2006, 86). Contrast this with the other extreme – the pervasive seven-day work-week culture in the high-tech and business communities.

We need to be aware of the different cultural models that may compete in our minds and cause confusion both in our inner worlds and in the social world. When we see the individual child in need of our protection as jurists or as helping professionals, we should not only be aware of and allow for the child's need to actualize his potential to be someone', to change and achieve. We should also foster or create the conditions necessary for him to simply be and feel unconditionally worthy and valued by society for who he is, for his present being.

The interplay between the need to be and the need to become is portrayed in Erik Erikson's brilliant biography of Mahatma Gandhi:

> We have seen that Gandhi was never too proud to find universal meaning in petty circumstances, for he knew that one must build on the values of one's childhood, as long as they are revalidated by experience, until one perceives a wider truth which may make them relative or obsolete.
>
> ERIKSON 1970, 398

The values Gandhi internalized in childhood were the building blocks of his being and the new truths he perceived allowed him to become the man he grew to be. Indeed, as explained in the first chapter of this essay, Gandhi exemplifies the dynamic reconstruction of identity. Erikson beautifully highlights and illustrates through the biography how the ability to reinvent oneself is solidly built on values of one's childhood constantly open to reinterpretation.

III Protecting the Child's Need to Be a Spiritually Authentic Being

The journey to becoming an authentic being can be a harrowing one. Nelson Mandela's personal and national struggle towards liberation is one such journey, of which he writes in his autobiography —The Long Walk to Freedom (Mandela 2002) The title and the narrative echo the exodus from Egypt. In the Jewish collective psyche, there is a place for a reading of the biblical narrative as one of a struggle to authenticity and resist the dominant culture. Rabbi Menachem Mendel Shneerson (the Lubavitcher Rebbe) explains:

> ... they [the Hebrew slaves in Egypt – Y.R.] retained their identity as Jews, preserved their uniqueness and kept up their traditions without anxiety or shame. It was this that assured their liberation from all forms of tyranny, physical and spiritual.
>
> SCHNEERSOHN 1996, 173

The author compares this to the frame of mind of assimilating Jews in twentieth-century America in a way that resonates closely with Taylor's concept of authenticity. He writes of the lost child, meaning the child who has no ties to his heritage:

> No Jewish child should be forgotten and given up. We must make every effort to save the lost child. Determined to do so and driven by a deep sense of compassion and responsibility, we need to have no fear of failure. To remedy any situation, we must discover its origins.

In this case, they lie in a mistaken analysis of their situation on the part of some immigrants arriving in a new and strange environment. Finding themselves a small minority, and encountering the inevitable difficulties of resettlement, some parents had the idea, which they communicated to their children, that assimilation was the solution. But in their efforts to abandon the Jewish way of life, they created a spiritual conflict within themselves. They were determined that their children should be spared the tension of divided loyalties. They looked for and therefore found faults with the Jewish way of life, while everything in the non-Jewish environment seemed attractive and good.

By this attitude, the parents hoped to ensure their children's survival in the new environment. But what kind of survival was it to be, if the soul was sacrificed for the material benefits of the world?

And what they thought was an escape into freedom turned out, in the final analysis to be an escape into slavish imitation, which tended to be so marked by caricature and a sense of insecurity as to command little respect from that younger generation that it was intended for (Schneersohn 1996, 172).

This passage, which I would title as the lost child passage, is instructive in several respects. First, it defines the assimilated child as a lost child. A child who has lost touch with his ancestral legacy, even if this is at his parents' initiative, is seen as lost. I suggest that this exemplifies how authenticity may go well beyond what the child knows and recognizes. It thus questions the limits of parental power in relation to the child's right to be one's self as part of a people and as part of a religious and cultural community.

The passage then moves us to question what survival is, what is freedom challenging a materialistic conception of survival, and of freedom as negative freedom; that is, freedom from constraints. Indeed the parents described aim to offer the child opportunities for material survival and prosperity; but is that enough to be free? The child is not offered the tools to authentically express his full unique potential as a human being, a being that has a spiritual dimension, a being that is more than the sum total of his material needs and desires.

Christman (2005) distinguishes between a conception of positive freedom as an internalized freedom to think and do and the commonplace conception of freedom as merely an absence of constraints. He explains why it is important to defend positive freedom:

> Those who want to cling to a positive conception of freedom of some sort insist that liberty should be seen as not merely an absence of constraints – whether those are considered as internal or external to the agent, the product of human action or accident, etc. Such theorists want to place the focus of our concern for liberty on the quality of agency and not merely the opportunity to act. Admitting that such a position may not be politically or morally neutral, defenders of such an understanding of freedom insist that merely establishing opportunities to act upon one's current desires fails to secure for citizens the conditions of authentic self-government that make freedom meaningful as an ideal. Seeing freedom as a quality of agency is different, conceptually, from seeing it as an absence of something. Autonomy is defined in various ways, but most conceptions stress the capacity for critical self-reflection in the development of value systems and plans of action. Such capacities do not merely emerge naturally, but must be developed through various processes involving educational, social, and personal resources. To see freedom as nothing more than the removal of certain interferences blinds us to the need for such resources, as well as their precise character, and so blinds us to the demands of just institutions.
>
> CHRISTMAN 2005, 79–88

The lost child passage highlights the spiritual component in authenticity that is marked by a willingness to pay a personal price for spiritual survival and freedom. According to the quoted passage, the child's need to be himself includes a need for a spiritual self, a need not to be enslaved to anyone's world view, and a need to be in touch with one's spiritual heritage in order to be able to be in dialogue with it and question it.

The author challenges the parent set on securing his child's survival with the notion that abandonment of a cultural heritage makes the child psycho-spiritually insecure. Thus, we are invited, through commitment to authenticity, to spiritualize our understanding of survival and freedom.

But is there a choice? That is, can one protect the child's need to be himself and neglect the spiritual component of the self and yet remain loyal to the humanity of human rights – to what makes us human and makes our rights and duties uniquely human? I claim that there is no choice. Protecting the child's need for a spiritually authentic being is essential if rights are to be exercised in a distinctly human way. Twerski's (2000) straightforward and clear explanation of the spiritual distinction between the animal and the human is helpful here:

> Human beings and animals both have biologic drives: hunger, thirst, sex, desire for comfort, avoidance of pain, and so on. However, animals are at the mercy of their biological drives and cannot resist them.
>
> Some psychologists would have us believe that our freedom of will is but an illusion. They argue that human beings have a number of drives, some of which are in conflict with others, and that human behavior is merely the result of the struggle among various drives for dominance.
>
> These psychologists may be in concert with those biologists who consider humans to be merely another variety of animal and according to this concept it is virtually meaningless to speak of spirituality.
>
> Our entire concept of human responsibility with our elaborate system of positive and negative sanctions, is based on the assumption that humans are not at the mercy of impulses and that we indeed have the freedom to choose and determine much of our behavior.
>
> Patrick Henry spoke for all humanity when he said – Give me liberty or give me death, as did the founding fathers when they asserted that man has an inalienable right to life, liberty and the pursuit of happiness. Tyranny is intolerable and is just as despicable when it is promoted by internal drives as when it is espoused by a ruthless despot. Slavery is abhorrent, not only because it is often cruel, but more so because it is dehumanizing. Human beings are free creatures and to take away our freedom is to rob us of our humanity.
>
> In contrast to animals, we need not be dominated by our biological drives. However, if a person avoids gratifying a given biological drive only out of fear of consequences, this person is still not behaving on a true human level because animals are also deterred by fear of

> punishment. When a decision to deny a biologic drive is based only on principles of right and wrong, a person rises to a supra animal level.
>
> TWERSKI 2000, 6–8

A child who has not been allowed the opportunity to develop a spiritual identity may see himself simply in terms of his drives. Such a child may become indifferent to his human rights or misuse them in a reductionist way to satisfy drives (Feuerstein and Hoffman 1982). Thus, exercise of rights may be divorced from theoretical rationales for human rights, that are distinctly supra animalistic (Twerski 2000; Cohn 1991, 17–43; Eekelaar 1994).

When adults strive to allow the child spiritual survival and freedom, he is able to rise to a supra animal level in exercising his rights.

IV Postmodernism and the Need to Be One's Self within a Committed Family that Offers the Child Values

Self-definition can never take place in a vacuum. A child knows who he is only within a specific familial and community context (Wilson 1997, 270, at 281–82), however dull at times. Besides being cared for, a child needs a familial and communal environment that he feels is his and that affords him a clear understanding of who he is and helps to give meaning to his life (Hassall 1994). The child's family and community are his starting points in life. Ideally, these are his, family and community of origin.

From within a family and its community, a child naturally begins to create meaningful ties and develop an identity that evolves over time. His experiences are gradually applied to new and widening fields beyond his family and community of origin as he matures biologically and emotionally.

The legal definition of family, however well informed by social science literature, is ultimately a value-laden cultural construction. Nevertheless, as explained in Chapter 1, legal rhetoric sometimes erroneously gives us the impression that such a legal definition captures some eternal factual truths.

It does capture truths, but they are moral rather than empirical truths. It is difficult to spell out these truths and stand up for them in the present-day postmodern climate. This climate threatens the future of human rights through the prevalent claim that there are no universal truths. For the family to protect the child's need to be, the family structure must reflect a deep connection between its members. Such a connection must be beyond a whimsical feeling, beyond an urge, beyond emotional upheaval (Steinsaltz 2001).

Thus, neither blood ties nor legal ties of parenthood necessarily represent psychological ties with a child that are worthy of state protection. To discover who fills the role of mother or father for the child, it is essential that recourse be made, among other things, to the child's subjective perceptions. In practical terms, protecting the child's need to be primarily means ensuring that he will not be forced to disown his authentic familial and communal identity, to the detriment of his sense of self and of his human dignity, in order to gain recognition of his normalcy by mainstream society (Bilsky 1997; Hassall 1994).

At the same time, we cannot evade the need to elucidate a universal truth that goes beyond the subjective and the individual case. For a secure protection of the child's need to be, we must curtail adult individualism.

In the words of Adin Steinseltz:

> Members of a family are bound by obligation, connected to each other by the knowledge that they can rely on each other (2001, 186).

The unfounded idea prevalent in western thought and public imagery of 'the abstract individual, detached from the collective bonds of history and sentiment' (Sacks 2005, 55) threatens the protection of the need to be.

The western world finds commitment to family difficult. That is why it is so important to base human rights on an ethos of care and interdependence, as proposed elsewhere (Brooks and Ronen 2006). Thus, the exercise of rights can potentially become truly responsive to children as whole human beings. Sacks's discussion sharpens the challenge we face today:

> Such a theory [a theory prevalent in Western popular culture that the self has no limits on what it can choose to do or be – Y.R.] certainly deconstructs the family. It robs it of its ethical foundations. At every stage, the idea of the family stands counter to the idea of unrestricted choice. To be a parent is to accept responsibility for a future I may not live to see. Families only exist on the basis of choices renounced.
>
> SACKS 2005, 56

I argue that precisely through renouncing their own freedom and accepting responsibility for a future they may not live to see, parents grant their children the freedom to create their own futures. Returning to Erikson's depiction of Gandhi, it is only when parents are present to offer values recognizable as the values of one's childhood can a Gandhi come into being. It is only then that the grown-up child can decide if his experience validates these values. Within a personal familial environment in which we find both commitment to values and personal space, the delicate interplay between the need to be and the need to become can take place in a way that promotes personal growth.

Parents in the postmodern world may be afraid of great truths.

The twentieth century led to disillusionment with the dogmatic ideologies that justified Nazi concentration camps and Soviet Gulags, but a post-traumatic anxious version of postmodernism destroys curiosity and vitality. As evidenced in the previous example of Gandhi's search, children become ethically and intellectually numb when there is no truth and no meaningful structural picture of the world. Why make the effort to study, know, and understand? (Goodman 2010, 334).

Through a historical perspective, Sacks offers a path of approaching great truths appreciatively and yet safely:

> Great truths bring good in their won domain and harm when they stray beyond it. Religion, the great truth about man's search for meaning, trespassed during the Middle Ages into two realms not its own: factual power and political power. The result was ignorance and persecution. This was why the Enlightenment was necessary. Liberalism, the great truth about coexistence in diversity, trespassed during the twentieth century into a neighboring field, morality, the great truth in living together in trust, and it too, brought harm, broken families, abandoned children, the 'new barbarism' of post-modernity. Extending beyond its scope, it threatened to destroy its own foundations … faced with the failure of libertarianism thinkers and activists alike rediscovered a truth that has become obscured: that we are and have our being in networks of belonging, which form the matrices of identity and moral purpose.
>
> SACKS 2000, 146, 172

Sacks speaks of the new barbarism of postmodernity. When Erich Fromm's classical and visionary book Escape from Freedom was first published during the Second World War, in 1941, the term postmodernity had not yet been coined. It therefore, fascinates me how his words are still relevant possibly in realms far beyond what he himself envisioned:

> The victory over all kinds of authoritarian systems will be possible only if democracy does not retreat but takes the offensive and proceeds to realize what has been its aim in the minds of those who fought for freedom throughout the last centuries. It will triumph over the forces of nihilism only if it can imbue people with a faith that is the strongest the human mind is capable of, the faith in life and in truth, and in freedom as the active and spontaneous realization of the individual self.
>
> FROMM 1994, 274

The language of not retreating, of taking the offensive and of fighting for freedom echoes a time of great anxiety for democracy and for freedom-loving people. It is written by a Jew of German descent who could not live and write as a free person in Germany and yet thinking well beyond the context of totalitarian regimes. Fromm speaks of our challenge of not escaping from the freedom that we have. I believe the justification for the strong language used is revitalized through our understandings of postmodernism. Democracy in the deep sense of the word is realized through the development of individuals. To the degree that we as adults regain our faith in truths, that we whole heartedly reject nihilism, despite the traumas of the 20th century, democracy will triumph through our children.

When children are in families that offer them values, they can feel protected in being who they are and have space to recreate themselves in fantasy and in real life. Children can dream their own dreams, wish their own wishes, and even carry out their own plans, irrespective of the small scale from which those dreams, wishes, and plans originate. Through interdependent relationships with their environment, children grow to be increasingly autonomous, yet never fully independent (See also Freeman 1997; Minow 1991; Fromm 1994; Hartling 2008).

The right to a self-constructed identity should not be like a castle flying in the air. Protection of the child's need to be oneself can be likened to protection of the foundations of a building, the building being one's identity. I have tried to explore here on a conceptual level how these foundations can be strengthened.

V Conclusion

In order for the child to fulfill his unique human potential, to arise to a supra animal motivation when exercising his rights, we must offer the child conditions for spiritual survival and for spiritual freedom, which include a tie to his heritage. For the family to protect the child's need to be himself, it also has to reflect a deep connection between family members that is often lacking.

Through renouncing their own freedom and accepting responsibility for a future they may not live to see, parents, standing counter to prevalent cultural trends, grant their children the freedom to create their own futures.

Furthermore, in order to prevent the ethical and intellectual numbing of their children, parents have to overcome the prevalent fear of great truths and offer their children the faith that there are truths to be discovered.

CHAPTER 5

The Courage to Hope and Protecting Children's Sense of Belonging: The Case of Child Protection

I Introduction

The main thesis of this chapter is that the decision, whether to allow an at-risk child and his kin the benefit of the doubt when prospective functioning, is value-laden and that decision-makers may be wrongly portrayed as skeptical and realistic. The chapter explores the implications of a willingness to entrust oneself, even momentarily, to the hopes of children at risk and their kin.

II On Skepticism and Reality

Nathan is a fourteen-year-old adolescent at risk; his father neglects him and his mother emotionally abuses him. He is exposed to a crumbling welfare system and to an excluding educational system His nineteen – old brother has been bullying him since he was a child. The parents turn a blind eye. In the last few months Nathan was involved in several violent incidents in school and was eventually expelled. He stole from the local community. Every inch of him is tied to his family and his community in a complex web of love-hate relationships.

Would we be wrong to open ourselves to Nathan and to his his family? Can we accept the problematic and blameworthy way they cope with life's challenges? Would it be unrealistic of us to commit ourselves to a relationship with them that facilitates revealing their suffering and merits to the general public and to ourselves professionally? Would we be foolish or wrong to hope for rehabilitating Nathan as part of a family and community meaningful to him?

In Western culture, the patronizing certainty of some decision-makers is closely tied to a rhetoric of critical skepticism. Such skepticism is considered more scientific, realistic, rational, and professional than truly questioning a dismal prognosis for the child at risk and having the courage to entrust oneself, even momentarily, to the hopes of at-risk children and their kin.

The chapter explains how willingness to give the disadvantaged individual the benefit of the doubt can create an environment in which professionals do not make dire predictions because they no longer see the individual's behavior at any given time as a predetermined fact. The subject matter of this chapter is

 | DOI 10.1163/9789004223677_006

related to the strengths perspective in the helping professions (see also Ronen 2005; Ronen and Ben Harush 2005).

Giving or receiving the benefit of the doubt engenders hope, and hope can empower the individuals, the families in emotional and functional distress, and even helping professionals. If an individual is given the benefit of the doubt, it relaxes the equation between that person's performance at a given moment and his potential (Bernitz 1999; Lazarus 1999; Mack 1999; Schudson 1999). Present-day Western culture values subjective certainty, which is often depicted and experienced as skepticism. Two contrasting conceptions can serve as a starting point for the professional's exploration of reality: she can regard different ideas concerning reality with impartial skepticism, or she can set out on her journey in virtually ingenuous wonderment regarding the subject matter of her exploration. Such wonderment precedes the formation of clear ideas that could become the objects of skepticism (Heschel 1983).

The skeptic aspiring to impartiality is predisposed to adhere to a positivist scientific approach. He strives to doubt everything. He believes that reality is concealed behind phenomena that are no more than impressions, or symbols, of reality (Levinas 1992). The aspiring skeptic believes that skepticism is a machless tool in scientific assessment, and that it will allow him to overcome preconceptions, superstitions, and despair.

However, reservations, which tend to dwarf and reject the Other, are not impartial criticism and cannot be an instrument of scientific thinking. Reservations overprotect us against disappointment and vulnerability. This kind of thinking cannot be pure scientific thinking.

When skepticism is used to judge others morally or socially, it may degenerate into dogmatism, since it tends to chip away systematically at the individual's motives and good intentions and to minimize the individual's ability to mend her ways and improve her behavior. If, when we judge others – for example, Nathan and his family – we adopt this pseudo-skeptical stance, it can lead to slothful thinking and action. We may begin to reason that if someone stumbles and is self-destructive or destructive towards others, there is no point in prolonged speculations about the feasibility of constructive change in the functioning of the individual and family or in professional work toward such a change (see also Levinas 1998).

We would therefore be hoodwinking ourselves if we thought of criticism as a tool for clarifying the truth. In the early twenty-first century, it is increasingly clear that David Wexler was right in his pioneering paper: we inhabit a culture of critique (Wexler 2000). In both the academic and legal worlds, it is accepted practice to approach people, their ideas, and their aspirations competitively.

We want to find 'what's wrong with them', and we feel diffident about surrendering to a belief, even as a brief experiment (Wexler, Stolle and Winick 2000). Many people in present-day Western society hesitate to admit a belief of any kind (Steinsaltz 2001). From that position, it is a short step to elevating critique of the Other to something sacred and regarding skepticism as indicating maturity and being grounded. Anyone yielding to trust, faith, or hope may be dismissed as gullible or naïve. Ingenuousness tends to carry negative connotations in Western society and is often equated with naïveté.

Furthermore, rigid dogmatic skepticism is liable to encourage moral apathy and, in extreme cases, even moral corruption. If the decision-maker's inner world is colored by a depreciating skepticism regarding himself and others, he can paint a portrait of society suggesting that a cynical view of evil is a necessary part of reality (Kook 1978; Kook 1992). It is no accident perhaps that demoralization refers both to loss of moral meaning and loss of hope (Sacks 2000). This hardening and unwillingness to allow others the benefit of the doubt becomes especially strong when the Other, for example, an adolescent in need of protection, such as Nathan, has a history of antisocial behavior

Orange explains how we may allow the Other the benefit of the doubt:

> If we assume that the other suffers from situations that are originally not of her or his making but has developed patterns of surviving that now look somewhere between quirky and insane, we may be more inclined to listen more closely. We may hear the cry of an abandoned child inside the raging adult or see the genuine despair in the face of the other who seems to be doing nothing for himself.
>
> ORANGE 2011, 65

Struggling families may collapse when professionals in positions of power give up hope (e.g. Featherstone, White and Morris 2014). A culture that does not facilitate yielding to faith in potential to do good has difficulty sustaining benevolent advocacy. In theoretical and public writing, and in the day-to-day work of child protection workers, child advocates, juvenile court and family court judges, a culture of critique has gained a powerful hold. It relegates the natural tendency for human compassion to one side. We are implicitly guided to prefer a reductionist, skeptical, dismissing worldview, which unjustly is considered the epitome of rationality and sound mindedness (Sacks 2000; Steinsaltz 2001; Tannen 1999; Wexler, Stolle and Winick 2000). The oversimplified world of cause and effect, in which an abused child is expected to return sooner or later to the attention of the child-protection system as an abuser, is liable to bring about the unjustified despair of helping professionals.

We suggest that we must dare to crystallize and believe in an evasive truth that calls for imagination, despite the temptation to cling to false certainties (Axline 1984; Kook 1992). I suggest that our consciousness does not conceal an unambiguous reality. Social reality can only be fully understood through subjective consciousness that does not evade recognition of ambiguity. Often, ambiguity is a natural given (Levinas 1992). Through language, we can imagine and envision a reality that is beyond what is perceived by our senses. The world to which may aspire through imagination may be different from the one we see, and in that sense we are uniquely human and moral (Sacks 2000).

It may be tempting in certain professional milieus to convince yourself and others that Nathan has psychopathic tendencies. This way, you can justify Nathan's social exclusion by placing him in a segregated institution for juvenile offenders, ostensibly for his own good. To imagine and believe that Nathan, harmed through abuse and neglect who has become abusive towards others, can alter his behavior, feel deeper empathy towards others, and act more empathetically, may take courage of imagination and vision. It may take even greater courage to claim that members of his nuclear or extended family can be seen as partners in his rehabilitation. Families and communities are not naturally trusted and respected for the good they can do for children in need of state protection (Featherstone, White and Morris 2014; Brooks and Ronen 2006; Bessel and Gal 2008; Cooper, Baistow, Hetherington, Pitts and Spriggs 1995). In short, the decision, whether to allow a child in need of protection and his family the benefit of the doubt is a value-laden decision.

Thus, it is important to recognize the inherent ambiguity and complexity in the lives of children at risk and their families. Recognition of ambiguity and complexity opens the door to hope. Hope challenges the professional to be courageous because it is different from optimism: we concede that progress and change are not inevitable, that we are taking a risk by hoping. At times, hope may empower us to believe in the potential of the child, who needs protection, and in the extended family, which struggles to respond to newly discovered needs in a situation of deprivation or abuse (Cooper, Baistow, Hetherington, Pitts and Spriggs 1995; Sacks 2000). By taking risks with the child and the extended family, and by allowing their narratives to be considered and respected, practitioners and policy makers can show a commitment to the child and family. They can bring new energy into a world that needs mending and protection to allow the child to thrive (Sacks 2000).

Therefore, when a child-protection worker or a judge is willing to express doubt about the threat, a law-offending boy poses or about impoverished parents' apathy toward their children's well-being, it is not a declaration of objective truth. Rather, the professional is setting subjective certainty aside and giving the child the benefit of the doubt. However, to the degree that professionals desire stability in their work environments and a greater sense of control in the lives of children and families under their protection, they may be liable to present their own subjective certainties as objective facts. A subjective certainty is not a truth but an illusion of the truth (Cohen 1992). Thus, the sense of stability and security, it may give the professional, is misguided.

The basis for a person not allowing himself and others the benefit of the doubt is irrational. The individual assumes that his deeds could ruin his fundamental nature and that they are evidence of his innermost motives. Naturally he will tend not to believe that his behavior can correct what is supposedly fundamentally wrong with him. These assumptions stem from a sometimes subconscious theory of personality.

It is ordinarily difficult to care for another person as a human being more than he cares for himself. It is still harder for the average person to see the good in the Other to the degree that he is accustomed to looking primarily at what is wrong with himself. If a person sees himself diminished by his own destructive actions, he will tend to diminish everyone else for such actions (Mindel 1985). Our position is tied to the postmodern critique of the self-confidence and authoritarianism of professionals rationalizing despair of the individual's capacity to change through recourse to the illusion of professional objectivity. However, postmodern thinking, especially to the extent that it supports ethical nihilism, may stem from a mood of cynicism. Thus a postmodern cultural climate may also foster despair of the human capacity for change and reparation.

The notions that a person's limitations are inherent and that their uniqueness is limited are accepted in the public discourse. An adolescent in Nathan's situation will be labeled violent rather than as having violent behavior, his father will be labeled neglectful rather than someone who was neglectful or who temporarily behaved neglectfully for explicit reasons. A youth who was caught stealing will be labeled as a law offender instead of being seen as someone who broke the law. An attractive and vulnerable girl who has run away from home after severe abuse from her parents to hang out penniless on an exotic beach, smoke marijuana, and engage in intimate relationships with strangers will often be seen as lacking inner boundaries, rather than as someone who has crossed boundaries in a way that is endangering her.

Legal culture and the professional culture of the helping professions interact with and mutually influence each other. The legitimate identification of inherent failings and faults in the family by helping professionals when they testify before the courts harms the child when these failings and flaws are treated, as though there were nothing significantly good to consider about family functioning. This is particularly so when such labeling serves the social end of excluding ostensive misfits and deviants from mainstream society. When helping professions are annexed by a legal tradition of purist liberal individualism, children's needs and suffering may be marginalized. Preoccupation with issues of evidence and procedure leaves little room for hope or envisioning a future that protects the child as a whole person whose identity and sense of belonging to a family and community are delicately evolving (see Brooks and Ronen 2006; Cooper, Baistow, Hetherington, Pitts and Spriggs 1995). Much of present-day professional discourse is based on an almost exclusive focus on abuse and problems and shows an inability or an unwillingness to recognize the capacity of children and their families to change.

In children's rights discourse it is common to address the rights of the child in the sense of the child's right to receive society's protection from being abused by his parents (Brooks and Ronen 2006). It is less common to find a discussion of the state's responsibility for the child as a young person rooted in the context of his family and community. Often, as I stated to explain in Chapter 1, rights discourse neglects social justice and the system-related injustices to young people and the disempowered families and communities to which they belong. A child who suffers violence has a right to be protected from violence, but she also has an often right to the protection of her significant ties (Freeman 2007). Nevertheless, the latter right is often neglected (Brooks and Ronen 2006) and she is stripped of meaningful components of her identity.

From a child-centered perspective, it is therefore, important not to concentrate exclusively on incidences of abuse and their prevention, but rather to see such prevention in a wider context of healing a relational world of a whole person who has a sense of belonging that is worthy of protection. Appropriately, and thoughtfully, allowing individuals in the family the benefit of the doubt regarding their capacity to change their behavior offers the child an opportunity to mend his family life. This can mean believing that family members can learn to refrain from abuse or neglect, or that they can learn how to shield the child from such behaviors perpetrated by others in the family. Alternatives to the family of origin, though sometimes vital to the child, are at best only the least detrimental alternative (Goldstein et al. 1996).

We have to draw a clear line between protecting the child as a whole person and protecting the interests of biological parents (Freeman 2007). Otherwise, rhetoric of family integrity and family values may serve to objectify children, allowing parents to 'love' them selfishly forsaking the children's needs and capacity for self-agency.

How should we treat the battered woman whose husband is violent towards her and to her children and who fails to protect her children from abuse? She may have the potential to become a good enough mother even when she is torn between a desire to stop the violence against her children and a desire to protect her children's right to belong to a community and a family that significant to them. It may be important to empower such a mother and encourage her to go to a battered women's shelter. However, she may find it hard to give up the only marital relationship she knows even for a short while. It is thus important for child protection professionals, whether helping or jurists, to converse with such a mother in a manner that demonstrates awareness of her failure to protect her children from physical abuse, other valid considerations she may have in remaining at home, and her potential to correct her maternal functioning. Acknowledging this potential gives hope to both the mother and the child. Naturally, in some cases, it is right to punish abusive or neglectful parents, and sometimes severe punishment is required. However, this is not the only child-protection scenario. From a child-centered perspective, the potential of the child-protection moral mandate is not exhausted in revealing abuse and neglect and penalizing those legally responsible for it. We cannot protect children as whole human beings when we ignore their sense of belonging. This poses a stiff challenge to both child-protection policymakers and practitioners.

III On Social Responsibility and the Public Response to Children at Risk and Their Families

The creation of a human rights regime with a strong declared commitment to the well-being of children followed the overdue recognition of the Other's vulnerability in societies that consider themselves civilized and enlightened. This human rights regime is a product of the twentieth century, a century in which million-and-a-half children and their families were slaughtered in the Jewish Holocaust and in which genocides continue. It has been called 'the century that knew no pity, gave no prize – not to the young, the weak, the innocent or the compassionate' (Segal 1999, 347). The cruelty we have witnessed this century utilized a rhetoric of state responsibility to the child. The greatest atrocities to children were done under the Hitlerian and Stalinist regimes which maintained- as befitting totalitarian regimes – that parents responsibility towards their children are no more than a form of their responsibilities towards society and the totalitarian State (Freeman 2007). However, we must be careful not to be irrationally fearful of state responsibility for the child because of these mass traumas. The international emergence of a human rights regime, which grew out of the ashes of World War II offers something new to the child. As explained in Chapter 3 above, this regime pledges responsibility for the treatment of children at risk and their families within a human rights context, we can allow ourselves to hope. Clearly, under such conditions, when a child finds himself in confrontation with society, it is vital to distinguish carefully between the risks to him because of this confrontation and the risks he poses to society because of it. It is vital to distinguish between a solution that serves the good of the youth as an individual and a solution that serves the good of the public, which includes the good of all young people. Failing to make this distinction we are liable to violate the child's right to a self-constructed identity and human dignity and slide down a slippery slope which leads us back to those regimes which confused between human rights and right of the people. It leads us back to the confusion between responsibility towards children per se and responsibility for children as no more than a form of responsibility to the state.

Though we claim that considering the child's good may serve the societal good, failing to recognize the tension between the different considerations that guide the framing and implementing of child-protection policies may be detrimental, particularly to youth: they may be penalized under the misleading pretext of helping them. This task of realizing the difference between protecting children and protecting society from children, particularly youth, is no simple one as it demands reflective practice (Kinsella 2010; Schon 1983), which is not common. However, even establishing this distinction cannot ensure that we will fulfill our undertaking to respect children and their families (Ronen and Ben Harush 2005).

Helping professionals must deal with expressions of narcissism in the therapy room. However, narcissism has moral implications beyond the narrow context of individual psychotherapy and psychodiagnosis. Like Narcissus, who fell in love with his own image, we are all liable to fall into the habit of adoring our own self-image. This is a common and human habit; it is healthy, to a degree. Thus, professionals should try to perceive narcissism in a broader, nonclinical sense. They should engage with the phenomena's social implications. They should identify the voices, pictures, and writings in which a person or group wraps and protects their individual identities in order to keep each one intact at all costs and to avoid real and painful exposure (Levinas 2010b; Epstein 2004).

When under pressure or stress, we may protect ourselves from acknowledging the suffering we cause others (Peck 1983). We thus preserve a pleasant but distorted image of our actions and treatment of others. This is, in some cases, a discrepancy between our image of how we treat children and the reality of their lives. A typical defensive tactic against criticism is to throw the ball back at the critic. When a professional adopts this defensive tactic, it can involve breaking down the critic's claims with an ad hominem rebuttal on the supposedly personality-based roots of social choices. However, though it may be true that the localities where we live and the social institutions, we are part of support and care for the child, it is also true that the more we lapse into narcissistic immaturity, the more the injustices to children at risk and their families become invisible and inaccessible. Imperviousness, unresponsiveness, and abuse directed toward children do not only happen in out-of-the-way places, in out-of-the-ordinary families, or among those labeled perverts and criminals; they happen in the public systems that were created to work for their well-being (Landsman 1974, 345–352) We are all human and prone to narcissistic failure.

As explained in Chapter 3, by choosing a fundamental allegiance to the disempowered – and children at risk and their families are more often that not disempowered – we share a responsibility to point out injustice, imperviousness, unresponsiveness, and abuse, wherever they occur, including in the child-protection systems themselves.

We cannot empower the disadvantaged and get on well with everyone else at the same time. Child protection practitioners and policymakers also do bad things to children and families, and it is certainly unpleasant to point an accusing finger at people within our collegial community. However, as Gandhi and professionals following his path explained and exemplified, unpleasantness and even confrontation can be a necessary price of social action that does not ascribe wrongdoing only to the disempowered and that believes in the reparability of the behavior of those who have not adjusted or found their place in society (Ronen 2004).

One cannot engage in professional work that promotes social change so long as a word such as 'injustice' is used to refer exclusively to the mental rubric of subjective experiences that the individual professional must process, dissect, and channel along paths of adjustment to the existing social order (Dayal 1986). No form of child-protection professional activity, among either legal or helping professionals, can be apolitical or amoral (Bellow 1996). I suggest that we still have a long way to go understandings are internalized in child protection practice.

Scientific exploration calls for imagination, and scientific understanding can be perceived as the product of a vibrant and frequently renewed combination of the ability to imagine and believe in new possibilities and the ability to think rationally. In order to integrate ideas from different spheres, critical thinking is not enough. We must seek out new insights, new points of view, new ways of thinking, and new knowledge.

In practice, despair and loss of motivation sometimes seize those who wish to dare and to believe, without, as it were, the vital crutch of theoretical knowledge, which is perceived to be scientific. Yet the postmodern era offers a scientific seal of approval for the view that the professional does not have a collection of true arguments regarding the world and the human world. Ignoring a person's inherent potential for change in the name of realism is a falsification of reality. It is precisely this view, which might cause negligence and carelessness when analyzing reality.

Just as scientific thinking calls for imagination and perceiving the alternatives, it is unthinkable for the justice system not to have faith in people. Even if we assigned a policeman to all those who do not believe the law is just to deter them from breaking it, we would not reach the degree of obedience typical of a society in which most of those subject to the law believe it is fundamentally just (Falk 1981). What complements the individual's belief in law's justness is society's faith in the individual, which may be reflected in legal norms and in the individual's ability to show care and consideration for his fellows, to dedicate himself to their needs and help them in improving their behavior. But if that is lacking, the justice system and helping professions who work within it cannot act effectively.

Thus, for example, Israeli law states both the rights and the duties of a child-protection worker: to launch proceedings to protect the child when he is physically or emotionally endangered by his parents, with a general provision not to remove the child from his parents' guardianship without exhausting alternative courses of action. How can we reconcile the two imperatives? How can a child not be removed from the parental home when her well-being is at risk and justifies state protection? Since it is widely agreed the child may not be seen as her parents' property, such provisions lead to the conclusion that the premise of the law is that parents can change. Parents who have failed in the way they treat their child are at times able and willing to mend their ways and show the child the love and devotion the law wishes to guarantee her. The lawmaker will therefore not accept professional intervention involving parents and families that reflects a general despair of the individual's inherent potential for improvement.

At times, the child maintains ties with extended family members and with the community that differ from those typical of the culture of most child-protection professionals. Many such children are excluded from the dominant culture and only have meager resources at their disposal. Understanding how these families and communities support their members and respecting these families is a great challenge. As I started to explain in Chapter 1, we are invited by the Convention and other international instruments to tackle this challenge. Thus, Article 5 of the Convention instructs the States to respect the responsibility of the extended family and community to guide the child in fulfilling his rights according to their culture.

Each of us is asked to make a genuine and ongoing effort to consider our incoherent assumptions. For example:

- What is sick or perverse in an individual's maladjustment to an unhealthy environment?
- What is normal in severe conditions of poverty and social injustice?
- What seems like an innately criminal and irredeemable personality, but, is in fact a personality developed under conditions that are almost impossible to survive and flourish in using normative too?

In such decisions incoherent assumptions may come into play.

IV Conclusion

This chapter opened with my narrative of Nathan's experience, which allowed us to unfold and demonstrate some of our observations, but how can we offer Nathan an opportunity to look ahead hopefully? It is common knowledge that in many societies, children like Nathan are not adequately protected against known risks to their well-being. If the condition of children at risk deteriorates within societies that declare their commitment to children's rights, as happens today in many countries, what is to be done?

So far, we have seen that, by giving individuals and families the benefit of the doubt, we can avoid perceiving negative predictions based on current behavior as solid facts. By giving them the benefit of the doubt, we can create hope, and hope can empower individuals and families who are in emotional and behavioral distress as well as the helping professionals involved with them professionally. I suggest raising awareness of the misguided equation of the limitations of the welfare system with the intrinsic limitations of the individual. I have explained that this position borders on ignorance of social injustices or a denial of their existence.

Courts may understand the observation that an adolescent addicted to alcohol or an emotionally deprived child is untreatable in the community to be a statement of fact reflecting solely on the nature or situation of the child in question. When this occurs, even helping professionals may feel hopeless, helpless, and isolated in their efforts to overcome these limitations unaided, and they can be tempted to see the limitations as permanent and intrinsic features of the young individual's life situation.

I propose that the personal situation of a child such as Nathan is largely a function of the poor standard of services available in many children's communities of origin. I have attempted to explore the possibility of redrawing the border between what is unrealistic, in terms of the individuals and the families in need of state protection, and what is or might become realistic. I assume, of course, that if appropriate efforts were invested in the individual and society, we could change what is classed as realistic.

The public agenda on child abuse may become distorted if abuses are hushed up when it is not politically correct to air them. Silent abuses, the mention of which is seen as a violation of political correctness, may include the abuse of foreign workers' children and families, refugees, and minority children. It may be difficult to oppose the current agenda because opposition undermines the balance of power. So what hope is there of avoiding the descent into social and personal irresponsibility?

Though it is true that failure hurts, failure in a healthy organism can encourage self-examination and self-criticism. No form of wisdom – not even selfish, survivalist wisdom – is achieved by rigidly protecting your self-image. Such protection amounts to enslavement and precludes responsiveness to the Other.

When individuals and social groups are affected by narcissism, there is an urge to silence and hide criticism that could mar ideal images. This can stifle a healthy desire to speak the truth. By silencing and hiding criticism, we can preserve our illusory self-love, but as I said, this image is a cover up for stagnation and lack of vitality. And it is on this score that we can raise people's awareness.

It may seem that we cannot avoid narcissistic behavior in our extroverted, achievement-oriented, Western individualist culture. Levinas (1990b) offers a counter-narrative to the Greek myth of Narcissus: a Talmudic narrative of a young shepherd who shaved the hair from his head when he noticed through looking at his image in the water how he was tempted to self-adoration.

Levinas writes:

> As the shepherd clearly saw, self-consciousness is the pride of the fool. Did he sense loosing himself when he gazed at himself?
>
> LEVINAS 1990B, 162

Levinas warns of the pride of the narcissist which he calls a fool. Following Levinas, we encourage a willingness to suffer the pain of our failures precisely in the context of children at risk and their families, those who's Otherness often arouses fear. If we are willing to accept that pain, it can help make our image of how we deal with children more realistic and increase our commitment to effective change. By reworking our attitude toward disadvantaged children, we can bolster society's moral strength. That strength stems from 'response ability', in other words, from seeing responsibility as an ability to respond to the needs of the Other (Sacks 2004).

We believe that professional communities that work with children should explore their social responsibilities and accept their role in shaping the public agenda. Even priorities for reform of child-protection policy led by children's Non-Governmental Organizations (hereafter: NGOs) may be distorted in a way that marginalizes children who are exposed to the worst abuses like sexual exploitation, hunger, and the lack of a secure home, since the weakest children are also the most voiceless and forgotten (Ronen and Ben Harush 2005). The silence, aloofness, refusal to take a stance, and even apathy that some academics or NGO workers show when they are faced with some of these abuses may be disguised as scientific-professional objectivity or realism.

For the child at risk to receive effective advocacy through both fieldwork and scholarly writing, we must commit ourselves to argue his case and dare to challenge social policy. It is unethical to work for children only on 'safe issues' – those issues that do not arouse strong opposition, and may even serve the organizational interests of advocacy organizations. Choosing only 'safe' issues betrays children. Academics, civil servants, and NGO workers share the responsibility to prioritize ethically between different child advocacy issues according to children's needs.

We can increasingly harness academic freedom to influence practice-oriented national debates on child-protection policy. We can achieve this by producing theoretical writing that is careful of false skepticism, overtly socially involved, and responsive to the concerns of children, parents and practitioners. As explained in Chapter 3, when we choose the subject matter and goals of our theoretical writing and public activism we should consider the trials of injustice and suffering that children and their families experience and bear in mind that these choices of ours cannot be amoral or apolitical. However, hard we might try to make them so, and though it may seem personally profitable for us as professionals to claim otherwise., the truth remains the same.

I expect that such writing and activism will highlight challenging insights and conclusions regarding the way we treat children and their families. Thus, it may offer them hope to actualize their full potential as interdependent human beings with dreams and hopes of their own. Through both academic writing and activism, we may promote a social reality in which a child such as Nathan can look ahead hopefully, a reality in which there is room for such dreams and hopes within families and communities of origin.

Endnote

We can grow through our writing. Through writing, our identity can continue to evolve at any age. Our writing also has a life of its own, it too can evolve on its own. It can continue to attract new meanings through others who consider and take to heart what matters to us and respond to it in different and unique ways (see also Suleiman 1994).

Gandhi, who has been influencing millions all over the world through his writing for decades after his death, writes of his experience:

> In my search for truth I have discarded many ideas and learnt many new things. Old as I am in age, I have no feeling that I have ceased to grow inwardly or that my growth will stop at the dissolution of the flesh. What I am concerned with is my readiness to obey the call of truth, my God, from moment to moment, and therefore, when anybody finds any inconsistency between any two writings of mine, if he has still faith in my sanity, he would do well to choose the latter of the two on the same subject.
>
> GANDHI, 1996, 2

I believe that both writing and reading are ideally be part of a process in which we discard ideas and embrace new learning embraced (for a moving portrayal of a personal intellectual journey see Rosen 2000, v–ix). I have tried to mindful of this potential in this book: Those of you who have read it may agree with me that the lessons I offer pertain to identifying challenges and questions, not so much to ultimate or conclusive answers, answers that leave little room for the reader's thoughtfulness and creative implementation.

Articulating relevant questions and challenges and offering a direction to respond to them is my principal aim in this work. I believe John Dewey, Albert Einstein and numerous others were right in suggesting great attention should be given to understanding a problem even at the expense of the attention given to formulating solutions to it (Campbell 1995, Couger 1995, 105)

I therefore chose not to conclude it by summarizing my proposals or by offering a call for action, though I am passionate about the subject-matter of this book.

I invite the reader to return to the text, to ponder whether and how her understanding of the child's right to identity has changed, how she now relates to children's sense of belonging, responsiveness to them and hope for them and maybe even to grow through the process.

 | DOI 10.1163/9789004223677_007

Bibliography

Alford, Fred C. 2007. "Levinas and the Limits of Political Theory", in *Levinas, Law, Politics*, edited by Marinos Diamatides, 107–123. New-York: Routledge-Cavendish.

Alston, Philip. 1994. "The Best Interests Principle: Towards a Reconciliation of Culture and Human Rights". *International Journal of Law, Policy and the Family* 8 (1): 1–25.

Alston, Philip, and Bridget Gilmour-Walsh. 1996. *The Best Interests of the Child: Towards a Synthesis of Children's Rights and Cultural Values*. Florence: UNICEF Innocenti Research Centre.

Anderer, Stephen, and David Glass. 2000. "A Therapeutic Jurisprudence and Preventive Law Approach to Family Law", in *Practicing Therapeutic Jurisprudence Law as a Helping Profession*, edited by Dennis Stolle, David Wexler and Bruce Winick, 207–234. Durham: Carolina Academic Press.

Anderson, Desmond M. 2006. *Proximity, Levinas and the Soul of Law*. Montreal: McGill-Queen's University Press.

An-Na'im, Abdullahi A. 2002. *Cultural Transformation and Human Rights in Africa*. London: Zed books.

An-Na'im, Abdullahi. 1994. "Cultural Transformation and Normative Consensus on the Best Interests of the Child". *International Journal of Law, Policy and the Family* 8 (1): 62–81.

Appiah, Anthony K. 1994. "Identity, Authenticity, Survival: Multicultural Societies and Social Reproduction", in *Multiculturalism: Examining the Politics of Recognition*, edited by Amy Gutmann, 149–164. Princeton: Princeton University Press.

Axline, Virginia. 1984. *Dibs: In Search of Self; Personality Development in Play Therapy*. Boston: Houghton Mifflin.

Bainham, Andrew. 2000. "Family Rights in the Next Millennium". *Current Legal Problems* 53 (1): 471–503.

Bala, Nicholas. 1999. "Report from Canada's Gender War Zone: Reforming the Child-Related Provisions of the Divorce Act". *Canadian Journal of family Law* 16: 163–227.

Barnes, Ashleigh. 2013. "The Trafficking of Children: A Counter-Narrative to the CRC's Construction of Care". *Socio-Legal Rev.* 9: 51–101.

Becroft, Andrew J. 2006. "Children and Young People in Conflict with the Law: Asking the Hard Questions". *Juvenile and Family Court Journal* 57: 1–37.

Bessell, Sharon, and Tali Gal. 2008. "Forming Partnerships: The Human Rights of Children in Need of Care and Protection". *International Journal of Children's Rights* 17: 1–16.

Bellow, Gary. 1996. "Steady Work: A Practitioner's Reflections on Political Lawyering". *Harvard Civil Rights-Civil Liberties* 31: 297–309.

Breznitz, Shlomo. 1999. "The Effects of Hope on Pain Tolerance". *Social Research* 66: 629–652.

Ben-Pazi, Chanoch. 2008. "The Levinasque Dialogue: Between Man and the Other, Between Dignity and Responsibility", in *Empowering Dialogues in Humanistic Education*, edited by Nimrod Aloni, 259–280. Tel Aviv: Hakibutz Hameuchad. Hebrew.

Bernasconi, Robert. 1988. "Failure of Communication as a Surplus: Dialogue and Lack of Dialogue between Buber and Levinas", in *The Provocation of Levinas: Rethinking the Other*, edited by Robert Bernasconi and David Wood, 100–135. London: Routledge.

Bilsky, Leora. 1997. "Naming and Re-Categorization in the Law". *The International Journal of Children's Rights* 5: 147–176.

Brighouse, Harry. 2002. "What Rights (if Any) do Children Have?", in *The Moral and Political Status of Children*, edited by David Archard and Colin M. Macleod, 31–52. New York: Oxford University Press.

Bloechal, Jeffry. 2000. *The Face of the Other and the Trace of God: Essays on the Philosophy of Emmanuel Levinas*, 143. New York: Fordham University Press.

Broeking, Julia, and Michele Peterson-Badali. 2009. "Parents' Involvement in the Youth Justice System: A View from the Trenches". *Canadian Journal of Criminology and Criminal Justice* 51 (2): 255–270.

Brooks, Susan, and Ya'ir Ronen. 2006. "The Notion of Interdependence and Its Implications for Child and Family Policy". *Journal of Feminist Family Therapy* 17: 23–46.

Bruch, Carol. 2001. "Parental Alienation Syndrome and Parental Alienation: Getting it Wrong in Child Custody Cases". *Family Law Quarterly* 35: 527–552.

Buckley, Fiona. 2002. "One Murder, Three Victims: James Bulger, Robert Thompson and Jon Venables". *Cork Online Law Review* [http://corkonlinelawreview.com/editions/2002/2002-10.pdf].

Burggraeve, Roger. 2002. *The Wisdom of Love in the Service of Love – Emmanuel Levinas on Justice, Peace and Human Rights*. Milwaukee: Marquette University Press.

Burggraeve, Rogers. 2007. *Alterity Makes the Difference. Ethical and Metaphysical Conditions for an Authentic Interreligious Dialogue and Learning*. Milwaukee: Marquette University Press.

Cahn, Naomi R. 1999. "Children's Interests in a Familial Context: Poverty, Foster Care, and Adoption". *Ohio State Law Journal* 60: 1189–1223.

Campbell, James. 1995. "Understanding John Dewey: Nature and Cooperative Intelligence". *International Studies in Philosophy*. Chicago: Open Court Publishing Company.

Cappelaere, Geert. 1995. *International Standards Concerning the Rights of the Child: United Nations Guidelines for the Prevention of Juvenile Delinquency (Riyadh Guidelines)*. Geneva: Defence for Children International.

Case of Brown vs. Board of Education of Topeka. 1954. 347 U.S. 483.

Case of Parham vs. J.R. 1979. 442 U.S. 584.

Case of T.V.U.K. (Application No. 24724/94) Judgment. 1999. Strasbourg.

Case of V.V.U.K. (Application No. 24888/94) Judgment. 1999. Strasbourg.

Case of R. v. Secretary of State, ex p V; R. v. Secretary of the Hume Department ex p T 1998. AC 409.

Christman, John. 2005. "Saving Positive Freedom". *Political Theory* 33 (1): 79–88.

Cohen, Stanley. 2001. *States of Denial: Knowing About Atrocities and Suffering*. Somerset: Wiley.

Cohen, Haim Herman. 1991. "A Human Rights Theory of Law: Prolegomena to a Methodology of Instruction", in *Haim H. Cohn: Selected Essays*, edited by Aharon Barak and Ruth Gabizon, 17–43. Tel Aviv: Bursi.

Cohen, Haim Herman. 1992. *The Law*. Jerusalem: Bialik Institute. Hebrew.

Collett, Steve. 1993. "Beyond Reason and Understanding – The Everyday Understanding of Crime". *Probation Journal* 40: 184–187.

Connolly, William. 1996. "Suffering, Justice and the Politics of Becoming". *Culture, Medicine and Psychiatry* 20: 251–277.

Cooper, Andrew, Karen Baistow, Rachel Hetherington, John Pitts and Angela Spriggs. 1995. *Positive Child Protection: A View from Abroad*. Lyme Regis: Russell House.

Couger, Daniel J. 1995. *Creativity and Innovation in Information Systems Organizations*. Danvers: Boyd and Fraser.

Cover, Robert M. 1998. "Violence and the Word", in *Narrative, Violence and the Law: The Essays of Robert Cover*, edited by Martha Minow, Michael Ryan and Austin Sarat, 203–238. Ann Arbor: University of Michigan Press.

Cutler, Karl E. 1994. *Runaway Me: A Survivor's Story*. Fort Collins: Blooming Press.

Daicoff, Susan. 2000. "The Role of Therapeutic Jurisprudence within the Comprehensive Law Movement", in *Practicing Therapeutic Jurisprudence: Law as a Helping Profession*, edited by Dennis P. Stolle, David B. Wexler and Bruce J. Winick, 465–492. Durham: Carolina Academic Press.

Dauer, Edward A. 2000. Foreword, in *Practicing Therapeutic Jurisprudence Law as a Helping Profession* by David Wexler, edited by Dennis P. Stolle, David B. Wexler and Bruce J. Winick, xiii–xiv. Durham: Carolina Academic Press.

Davidovitch, Nadav, and Michal Alberstein. 2008. "Therapeutic Jurisprudence and Public Health: A Broad Perspective on Dialogue". *Thomas Jefferson Law Review* 30 (2): 507–524.

Davidson, Howard. 1995. "Child Abuse and Domestic Violence; Legal Connections and Controversies". *Family Law Quarterly* 29 (2): 357–373.

Dayal, Parmeshwari. 1986. *Gandhian Approach to Social Work*. Ahmedabad: Navajivan.

Delgado, Richard. 1989. "Storytelling for Oppositionists and Others: A Plea for Narrative". *Michigan Law Review* 87 (8): 2411–2441.

Deng, Francis, and General Olusegun Obasanjo. 2000. "Conclusion: The Cause of Justice Behind Civil Wars", in *The Politics of Memory: Truth, Healing and Social Justice*, edited by Ifi Amadiume and Abdullahi An-Nain, 184–200. London: Zed Books.

Downing, Kevin. 1994. "When Children Commit Murder, Who is Really Responsible?" *Justice of the Peace and Local Government Law* 158: 51–52.

Eberle, Edward J. 2002. *Dignity and Liberty: Constitutional Visions in Germany and the United States*. Westport: Praeger.

Eekelaar, John. 1994. "The Interests of the Child and the Child's Wishes: The Role of Dynamic Self-Determinism". *International Journal of Law, Policy and the Family* 8 (1): 42–61.

Eekelaar, John. 2004. "Children between Cultures". *International Journal of Law, Policy and the Family* 18 (2): 178–194.

Engel, David M. and Frank W. Munger. 1996. "Rights, Remembrance, and the Reconciliation of Difference". *Law and Society Review* 30 (1): 7–53.

Ennew, Judith. 1998. "Shame and Physical Pain: Cultural Relativity, Children, Torture and Punishment", in *Childhood Abused: Protecting Children against Torture, Cruel, Inhuman and Degrading Treatment and Punishment*, edited by Geraldine Van Bueren, 7–34. Farnham: Ashgate.

Epstein, Daniel. 2004. "Endnote: From Ithaca to Ethics", in *New Talmudic Readings*, by Emmanuel Levinas. 97–133. Jerusalem: Schoken. Hebrew.

Erikson, Erik H. 1963. "The Golden Rule and the Cycle of Life", in *The Study of Lives: Essays on Personality in Honor of Henry A. Murray*, edited by Robert W. White and Katherine F. Bruner, 412–428. New York: Atherton Press.

Erikson, Erik H. 1970. *Gandhi's Truth: On the Origins of Militant Nonviolence*. New York: Norton.

Fagenblat, Michael. 2010. *A Covenant of Creatures: Levinas's Philosophy of Judaism*. Stanford: Stanford University Press.

Falk, Ze'ev. 1981. *Law and Religion: The Jewish Experience*. Jerusalem: Mesharim.

Feast, Julia and David Howe. 2000. *Adoption, Search and Reunion: The Long Term Experience of Adopted Adults*. London: Children's Society.

Featherstone, Brid, Sue White, and Kate Morris. 2014. *Re-imagining Child Protection: Towards Humane Social Work with Families*. Bristol: Policy Press.

Federle, Katherine H. 1990. "The Abolition of The Juvenile Court: A Proposal for The Preservation of Children's Legal Rights". *Journal of Contemporary Law* 16 (1): 23–52.

Ferguson, Robert A. 1996. "Untold Stories in the Law", in *Law's Stories: Narrative and Rhetoric in the Law*, edited by Peter Brooks and Paul Gewirtz, 84–98. New Haven: Yale University Press.

Feuerstein, Reuven. 1984. *On the Desirability of Preserving Family and Communal Traditions*. Jerusalem: Jewish Agency.

Feuerstein, Reuven, and Mildred B. Hoffman. 1982. "Intergenerational Conflict of Rights: Cultural Imposition and Self-Realization". *Viewpoints in Teaching and Learning* 58 (1): 44–63.

Finley, Lucinda. 1986. "Transcending Equality Theory: A Way out of the Maternity and Workplace Debate". *Columbia Law Review* 86 (6): 1118–1182.

Fortin, Jane. 1998. *Children's Rights and the Developing Law*. London: Butterworths.

Franklin, Bob. 1986. "Children's Political Rights", in *The Rights of Children*, edited by Bob Franklin, 24–53. Oxford: Blackwell.

Freeman, Michael. 1997. *The Moral Status of Children: Essays on the Rights of the Child*. The Hague: Martinus Nijhoff Publishers.

Freeman, Michael. 2007. "Article 3. The Best Interests of the Child", in *A Commentary on the United Nations Convention on the Rights of the Child* by Andre Alen, Johan Vande Lanotte, Eugene Verhellen, Fiona Ang, Eva Berghmans, and Mieke Vereyde. Leiden: Martinus Nijhoff.

Fromm, Erich. 1994. *Escape from Freedom*. New York: Holt.

Frowein, Jochen Abraham. 2002. "The Concept of Human Dignity in International Law", in *The Concept of Human Dignity in Human Rights Discourse*, edited by David Kretzmer and Eckart Klein, 121–132. Hague: Martinus Nijhoff Publishers.

Fuller, Robert W. 2006. *All Rise: Somebodies, Nobodies, and the Politics of Dignity*. San Francisco: Berrett-Koehler Publishers.

Gal, Tali and Vered Shidlo-Hezroni. 2011. "Restorative Justice as Therapeutic Jurisprudence: The Case of Child Victims", in *Therapeutic Jurisprudence and Victim Participation in Justice: International Perspectives*, edited by Edna Erez and Michael Kilchling, 139–167. Durham.

Gandhi, Mohandas Karamchand. 1994. *An Autobiography or the Story of My Experiments with Truth*, translated by Mahadev Desai. Ahmedabad: Navajivan.

Gandhi, Mohandas Karamchand. 1996. *The Mind of Mahatma Gandhi*, compiled and edited by R.K. Prabhu and U.R. Rao. Navajivan: Ahmedabad.

Geertz, Clifford. 1983. *Local Knowledge: Further Essays in Interpretative Anthropology*. New York: Basic Books.

Gilat, Israel Zvi. 2015. "On the Path of Late Prof. Menachem Elon in Empowering Jewish Law: Parent–Child Relationships as a Parable". *Hakira, the Flatbush Journal of Jewish Law and Thought* 19: 5–34. Hebrew.

Gilligan, Carol. 1982. *In a Different Voice: Psychological Theory and Women's Development*. Cambridge: Harvard University Press.

Goldstein, Joseph, Albert J. Solnit, Sonja Goldstein, and Anna Freud. 1996. *Best Interests of the Child: The Least Detrimental Alternative*. New-York: Free Press.

Goldstein, Joseph. 1975. "Why Foster Care? – for Whom, for How Long?" *Psychoanalytic Study of the Child* 30: 642–647.

Goodman, Micah. 2010. *The Secrets of the Guide to the Perplexed.* Jerusalem: Dvir. Hebrew.

Guggenheim, Martin. 2000. "Somebody's Children: Sustaining the Family's Place in Child Welfare Policy", in *Review of Nobody's Children: Abuse and Neglect, Foster Drift, and the Adoption Alternative*, by Elizabeth Bartholet. *Harvard Law Review* 113 (7): 1716–1750.

Hall, Jennifer. 1992. "Psychological-mindedness: A conceptual Model". *American Journal of Psychotherapy* 46 (1): 131–140.

Haley, Joseph R. 1991. *Black's Law Dictionary.* Eagan: West Publishing Company.

Hammerschlag, Sarah. 2010. *The Figural Jew: Politics and Identity in Postwar French Thought.* Chicago: University of Chicago Press.

Hannah-Jones, Nikole. 2014. School Segregation, the Continuing Tragedy of Ferguson: Michael Brown beat the odds by graduating from high school before his death – odds that remain stacked against black students in St. Louis and the rest of the country. *ProPublica,* December 19, 2014. [http://www.propublica.org/article/ferguson-school-segregation] (retrieved 12.8.15).

Harris, Cyril. 2001. *For Heaven's Sake.* London: Valetine Mitchell.

Hartling, Linda. 2008. "Strengthening Reselience in a Risky World: It's All about Relationships". *Women and Therapy* 31 (2–4): 51–70.

Hassall, Ian B. 1994. *The Child's Right to a Place, but Whose Place?* Wellington: Office of the Commissioner for Children.

Heneman, Dori. 2006. "What Does India Add to the Teachings of the Land of Israel: Musings of an Educator", in *From India Till Here,* edited by Nir Elhanan, 79–80. Jerusalem: Rubin Mass.

Heschel, Abraham Joshua. 1951. *The Sabbath: It's Meaning for Modern Man.* New York: Farrar, Straus and Giroux.

Heschel, Abraham Joshua. 1983. *God in Search of Man: A Philosophy of Judaism.* New York: Farrar Straus and Giroux.

Hodgson, Douglas. 1993. "The International Legal Protection of the Child's Right to a Legal Identity and the Problem of Statelessness". *International Journal of Law and the Family* 7 (2): 255–270.

Hom, Sharon K., and Eric K. Yamamoto. 1999. "Collective Memory, History, and Social Justice". *UCLA Law Review* 47: 1747–1802.

Jackson, David. 1995. *Destroying the Baby in Themselves: Why Did the Two Boys Kill James Bulger?* Nottingham: Mushroom Publications.

Jefferson, Tony. 1996. *The Sleep of Reason: The James Bulger Case – Review of Destroying the Baby in Themselves: Why Did the Two Boys Kill James Bulger?*, by David James Smith. London: Arrow, 1995.

Kant, Immanuel. 2004. *Critique of Practical Reason.* New York: Dover and Newton Abbot.

Kaplan, Yehiel. 2002. "Children's Rights in Israeli Law: The Beginnings of the Shift from Paternalism to Autonomy". *Hamishpat* 7: 303–334.

Kaplan, Yehiel. 2001. "From the Child's Best Interests to the Child's Rights". *Mishpatim, The Hebrew University Law Review* 31: 623–692.

Katz, Claire. 2010. "Education East of Eden: Levinas, the Psychopath, and the Paradox of Responsibility", in *Radicalizing Levinas*, edited by Peter Atterton and Matthew Calarco, 171–183. Albany: SUNY Press.

Keddell, Emily. 2011. "Reasoning Processes in Child Protection Decision Making: Negotiating Moral Minefields and Risky Relationships". *British Journal of Social Work* 41.7: 1251–1270.

Kilkelly, Ursula. 1999. *The Child and the European Convention of Human Rights*. Aldershot: Dartmouth.

King, Michael S. and CL (Lou) Tatasciore. 2006. "Promoting Healing in the Family; Taking a Therapeutic Jurisprudence Approach in Care and Protection Applications". *eLaw Journal: Murdoch University Electronic Journal of Law. Special Issue: The Therapeutic Role of Magistrates' Courts*: 78–94.

King, Michael and Judith Trowell. 1992. *Children's Welfare and the Law*. London: Sage.

Kinsella, Elizabeth Anne. 2010. "The Art of Reflective Practice in Health and Social Care: Reflections on the Legacy of Donald Schön". *Reflective Practice* 11 (4): 565–575.

Kleinman, Arthur. 1996. "Suffering, Ethics, and the Politics of Moral Life". *Culture, Medicine and Psychiatry* 20: 287–290.

Kline, Marlee. 1992. "Child Welfare Law, 'Best Interests of the Child', Ideology and First Nations". *Osgoode Hall Law Journal* 30 (2): 375.

Kook, Abraham Hacohen. 1978. *The Lights of Penitence: The Moral Principles*, edited and translated by Bokser Ben Zion. New York: Paulist Press.

Kook, Abraham Isaac. 1992. *Lights of Holiness*, Vol. 1. Jerusalem: Rav Kook Institute. Hebrew.

Koptiuch, Kristin. 1996. "Cultural Defense and Criminological Displacements: Gender, Race and Nation in the Legal Surveillance of US Diaspora Asians", in *Displacement, Diaspora and Geographies of Identity*, edited by Smadar Lavie and Ted Swedenburg, 215–233. Durham: Duke University Press.

Korbin, Jill E. 1994. "Sociocultural Factors in Child Maltreatment", in *Protecting Children from Abuse and Neglect – Foundations of a New National Strategy*, edited by Gary Melton and Frank Barry, 182–223. New-York: Guilford Publications.

Korbin, Jill E. 2002. "Culture and Child Maltreatment: Cultural Competence and Beyond". *Child Abuse and Neglect* 26: 637.

Krumer-Nevo, Michal and Menny Malka. 2012. "Identity wounds: Multiple Identities and Intersectional Theory in the Context of Multiculturalism", in *Navigating*

Multiple Identities: Race, Gender, Culture, Nationality and Role, edited by Edith R. Josselson and M. Harway, 187–206. New-York: Oxford University Press.

Kufeldt, Kathleen. 1993. "Listening to Children: An Essential for Justice". *International Journal of Children's Rights* 1 (2): 133–155.

Kunz, George. 1998. *The Paradox of Power and Weakness*. Albany: State University of New York Press.

Kymlicka, Will. 1989. *Liberalism, Culture and Community*. New York: Oxford University Press.

Landsman, Ted. 1974. "The Humanizer". *American Journal of Orthopsychiatry* 44: 345–352.

Lavie, Smadar and Ted Swedenburg. 1996. *Displacement, Diaspora, and Geographies of Identity*. Durham: Duke University Press.

Lazarus, Richard. 1999. "An Emotion and a Vital Coping Resource against Despair". *Social Research* 66: 653–678.

Levinas, Emmanuel. 1988. "Useless Suffering", in *The Provocation of Levinas: Rethinking the Other*, edited by Robert Bernasconi and David Wood, 156–165. London: Routledge.

Levinas, Emmanuel. 1990a. "Judaism and Revolution", in *Nine Talmudic Readings*, by Emmanuel Levinas, translated by Annette Aronowicz, 94–119. Bloomington: Indiana University Press.

Levinas, Emmanuel. 1990b. "The Youth of Israel", in *Nine Talmudic Readings*, 120–135. Bloomington: Indiana University Press.

Levinas, Emmanuel. 1990c. "Toward the Other", in *Nine Talmudic Readings*, 12–29. Bloomington: Indiana University Press.

Levinas, Emmanuel. 1992. "The Phenomenological Theory of Being", in *The Levinas Reader*, 11–28. Oxford: Basil Blackwell.

Levinas, Emmanuel. 1996. "Transcendence and Height", in *Basic Philosophical Writings*, edited by Adrian Peperzak, Siomon Critchley and Robert Bernasconi, 11–32. Bloomington: Indiana University Press.

Levinas, Emmanuel. 1997. *Difficult Freedom: Essays on Judaism*, translated by Sean Hand. Baltimore: John Hopkins University Press.

Levinas, Emmanuel. 1998. "Uniqueness", in *Entre nous: On Thinking-of-the-Other*, 189–197. New York: Columbia University Press.

Levinas, Emmanuel. 2003. *Totality and Infinity: An Essay on Exteriority*, translated by Edit Alphonso Lignis. Pittsburgh: Duquesne University Press.

Levinas, Emmanuel. 2004. *New Talmudic Lectures*, translated from French by Daniel Epstein. Jerusalem: Schocken. Hebrew.

Lewis, Anthony. 1998. Comment, in *Work and Welfare by Robert Solow*, edited by Amy Gutman, 55–62. Princeton: Princeton University Press.

Lichtenstein, Tovah. 1991. "The Decision-Making Process of Removing a Child from the Home; Covert and Overt Influences". *Society and Welfare* 11 (2): 117–126.

Lindner, Evelin. 2009. *Emotion and Conflict: How Human Rights Can Dignify Emotion and Help Us Wage Good Conflict*. Westport: Praeger Publishers.

Lindner, Evelin. 2012. *A Dignity Economy: Creating an Economy that Serves Human Dignity and Preserves Our Planet*. Lake Oswego: Dignity Press.

Love, B.J. 2004. "Brown Plus 50 Counter-Storytelling: A Critical Race Theory Analysis of the 'Majoritarian Achievement Gap' Story". *Equity & Excellence in Education* 37 (3): 227–246.

Lukinsky, Joseph. 1987. "Law in Education: A Reminiscence with Some Footnotes to Robert Cover's Nomos and Narrative". *The Yale Law Journal* 96 (8): 1836–1859.

Lyon, Christina and Peter De Cruz. 1993. *Child Abuse*. Bristol: Jordan Publishing.

Mack, Aricn. 1999. "Liberty and Pluralism – Editor's Introduction". *Social Research* 66 (4): iii–iv.

Madden, Robert and Rayme Wayne. 2003. "Social Work and the Law: A Therapeutic Jurisprudence Perspective". *Social Work* 48 (3): 338–347.

Malcolm, David. 2007. "Addressing Juvenile Crime by Fixing the Dysfunctional Family". *University of Notre Dame Australia Law Review* 9: 19–45.

Mandela, Nelson. 2002. *Long Walk to Freedom: The Autobiography of Nelson Mandela*. London: Abacus.

Maruna, Shad. 2001. *Making Good: How Ex-Convicts Reform and Rebuild Their Lives*. Washington D.C: American Psychological Association.

McBride, Jeremy. 1998. "The Violation of Economic, Social and Cultural Rights as Torture or Cruel, Inhuman or Degrading Treatment", in *Childhood Abused: Protecting Children Against Torture, Cruel, Inhuman and Degrading Treatment and Punishment*, edited by Geraldine Van Bueren, 107–116. Farnham: Ashgate.

McCamey, Jimmy. 2010. "Reducing Recidivism in Adolescent Sexual Offenders by Focusing on Community Reintegration". *Residential Treatment for Children and Youth* 27 (1): 55–67.

Meriwether, Margaret. 1986. "Child Abuse Reporting Laws: Time for a Change". *Family Law Quarterly* 20 (2): 141–171.

Melton, Gary. 1992. "The Law is a Good Thing (Psychology is, Too): Human Rights in Psychological Jurisprudence". *Law and Human Behavior* 16 (4): 381–398.

Melton, Gary. 1994. "Is There a Place for Children in the New World Order", in *Justice For Children*, edited by Stuart Asquith and Malcolm Hill, 26–58. The Hague: Martinus Nijhoff Publishers.

Melton, Gary B. and Gail S. Perry. 1984. "Precedential Value of Judicial Notice of Social Facts: Parham as an Example". *Journal of Family Law* 22 (4): 633–676.

Mindel, Nissan. 1985. *The Philosophy of Chabad*. New York: Kehot.

Minow, Martha. 1987. "We, the Family: Constitutional Rights and American Families". *The Journal of American History* 74 (3): 959–983.

Minow, Martha. 1990. "Words and the Door to the Land of Change: Law, Language, and Family Violence". *Vanderbilt Law Review* 43: 1665–1699.

Minow, Martha. 1991. *Making All the Difference: Inclusion, Exclusion and American Law*. Ithaca: Cornell University Press.

Minow, Martha. 1996. "Comments to Suffering, Justice and the Politics of Becoming by William E. Connoley". *Culture, Medicine and Psychiatry* 20: 279–286.

Minow, Martha. 1999. *Between Vengeance and Forgiveness: Facing History after Genocide and Mass Violence*. Boston: Beacon Press.

Mody, Sanjay. 2004. "Note: Brown Footnote Eleven in Historical Context: Social Science and the Supreme Court's Quest for Legitimacy". *Stanford Law Review* 54: 793–829.

Morgan, Alice. 2006. "The Position of the Therapist in Working with Children and Families", in *Narrative Therapy with Children and Their Families*, edited by Michael White and Alice Morgan, 57–84. Adelaide: Dulwich Center Publications.

Mundlak, Guy. 2003. "Neither Insiders nor Outsiders: The Contractual Construction of Migrant Workers' Rights and the Democratic Deficit". *Iyunei Mishpat, Tel Aviv University Law Review* 27: 423–487.

Nandy, Ashis. 1990. *At the Edge of Psychology: Essays in Politics and Culture*. Oxford: Oxford University Press.

Nandy, Ashis. 2004. *Traditions, Tyranny and Utopias: Essays in the Politics of Awareness*, 54–62. New Delhi: Oxford University Press.

Novoa, Ana M. 1999. "Count the Brown Faces: Where is the Family in the Family Law of Child Protective Services". *Scholar* 1: 5–43.

Olsen, Frances E. 1985. "The Myth of State Intervention in the Family". *Michigan Journal of Law Reform* 18: 835–864.

Orange, Donna. 2011. *The Suffering Stranger: Hermeneutics for Everyday Clinical Practice*. New York: Routledge.

Peck, Scott M. 1983. *People of the Lie: The Hope for Healing Human Evil*. New York: Simon and Schuster.

Perlin, Michael L. 2000. "A Law of Healing". *68 U. Cin. L. Rev.*: 407.

Perlin, Michael L. 2004. "'Salvation' or a 'Lethal Dose'? Attitudes and Advocacy in Right to Refuse Treatment Cases". *Journal of Forensic Psychology Practice* 4 (4): 51–69.

Post, Robert. 1995. *Constitutional Domains: Democracy, Community, Management*. Cambridge: Harvard University Press.

Raz, Joseph. 1998. "Multiculturalism". *Ratio Juris* 11 (3): 193–205.

Reifen, David. 1978. *The Minor and the Juvenile Court*. Tel Aviv: Hakibutz Hame'euchad.

Roberts, Dorothy E. 1999. "Is There Justice in Children's Rights? The Critique of Federal Family Preservation Policy". *University of Pennsylvania Journal of Constitutional Law* 2 (1): 126–127.

Rogers, Carl R. 1989. *Carl Rogers on Personal Power*. London: Constable.

Ronen, Ya'ir. 1997. *The Child's Participation in the Determination of His Guardianship*. Tel-Aviv: Bursi Legal Publishers.

Ronen, Ya'ir. 1998. "Protection for Whom and from What? Protection Proceedings and the Voice of the Child at Risk", in *Children's Rights and Traditional Values*, edited by Gillian Douglas and Leslie Sebba, 249–263. Farnham: Ashgate Publishing Ltd.

Ronen, Ya'ir. 2004a. "Child Advocacy as an Effort to Swim against the Tide", in *Global Perspectives on Creative Child Advocacy*, edited by Susan Brooks and Ved Kumari, 285–300. Thousand Oaks: Sage.

Ronen, Ya'ir. 2004b. "Redefining the Child's Right to Identity". *International Journal of Law, Policy and the Family* 18 (2): 147–177.

Ronen, Ya'ir. 2005a. *Advocacy for the Child as a Tool for Social Change*, edited by Aharon Barak, Israel Zvi Gilat, Sinay Deutsch, and Hadara Bar-Mor. *Law Review of Netanya Academic College Law School – Special Issue in Honor of Prof. Avner H. Shaki* 26: 617–638.

Ronen, Ya'ir. 2005b. "On the Strengths of the Child and His Family in a Legal Context", in *Maximizing Capacities Applications of the Strengths Perspective in Social Work*, edited by Ben-Zion Cohen and Eli Buchbinder, 133–156. Tel Aviv: Ramot, Tel Aviv University Press.

Ronen, Ya'ir. 2006. "The Construction of Memory through Law and the Law's Responsiveness to Children". *Law and Psychology, Current Legal Issues* 9: 406–429.

Ronen, Ya'ir. 2008a. "An Introductory Note on Law's Responsiveness to the Child's Suffering and the Construction of a Child Advocacy Agenda", in *The Case for the Child: Towards the Construction of a New Agenda*, edited by Ya'ir Ronen and Charles W. Greenbaum, 39–44. Antwerp: Intersentia.

Ronen, Ya'ir. 2008b. "On Suffering and the Voices of Real Children in Israeli Law", in *Social Exclusion and Human Rights in Israel*, edited by Ya'ir Ronen, Israel Doron and Vered Slonim-Nevo, 37–171. Tel Aviv: Ramot, Tel Aviv University Press.

Ronen, Ya'ir and Yaniv Ben Harush. 2005. "The Legal Treatment of Youth: Between Reality and Prevalent Conceptions", in *Youth in Israel*, edited by Yohanan Wozner and Giora Rahav, 207–246. Tel Aviv: Interdisciplinary Center for the Study of Child and Youth Policy and Treatment, Tel Aviv University.

Ronen, Ya'ir and Charles W. Greenbaum. 2008. "Introduction: A New Agenda for Children: Making Progress in the Future after Mixed Success in the Past", in *The Case for the Child: Towards a New Agenda*, edited by Ya'ir Ronen and Charles W. Greenbaum, 1–11. Antwerp: Intersentia.

Rosen, Jeremy. 2000. *Exploding Myths that Jews Believe*. Northvale: Jason Aronson.

Rosenblatt, Jeremy. 1996. "The Needs of Black and Ethnic Children". *Family Law* 26: 641–642.

Rotenberg, Mordechai. 1987. *Re-Biographing and Deviance: Psychotherapeutic Narrativism and the Midrash.* New York: Praeger Publishers.

Ryan, Scott D., Gardenia Harris, Donna Brown, Doris M. Houston, Susan Livingston Smith, and Jeanne A. Howard. 2011. "Open Adoptions in Child Welfare: Social Worker and Foster/Adoptive Parent Attitudes". *Journal of Public Child Welfare* 5 (4): 445–466.

Sacks, Jonathan. 1995. *Faith in the Future.* London: Darton, Longman and Todd.

Sacks, Jonathan. 2000. *The Politics of Hope.* London: Vintage Books.

Sacks, Jonathan. 2002. *The Dignity of Difference: How to Avoid the Clash of Civilizations.* New York: Continuum.

Sacks, Jonathan. 2004. "Noach: A Drama in Four Acts". Last modified November 1st 2008: [http://www.rabbisacks.org/covenant-conversation-5769-noach-a-drama-in-four-acts] (Accessed August 11, 2016).

Sacks, Jonathan. 2005. *The Persistence of Faith: Religion, Morality and Society in a Secular Age.* London: Continuum.

Sebba, Leslie. 1992. "Judging Youths – Or Judging Their Offenses?" *Mishpatim, The Hebrew University Law Review* 21 (3): 570–575.

Schneersohn, Mendel M. 1996. *Torah Studies: Discourses*, adapted by Jonathan Sacks. New York: Kehot Publication Society.

Schön, Donald A. 1983. *The Reflective Practitioner: How Professionals Think in Action.* London: Temple Smith.

Schuz, Rhona. 2015. "Dangers of Children's Rights' Discourse in the Political Arena: The Issue of Religious Male Cicumcision as a Test Case". *The Cardozo Journal of Law and Gender* 21: 347–391.

Schorr, Nanette. 1993. "Foster Care and the Politics of Compassion", in *Family Matters: Readings on Family Lives and the Law*, edited by Martha Minow, 117–124. New York: The New Press.

Sharon, Eli. 1998. *Minors at Risk: Judgment, Treatment and Supervision in the Juvenile Court.* Netanya: Institute for Studies of Law and Economics.

Sheehan, Katherine. 2000. "Caring for Deconstruction". *Yale Journal of Law and Feminism* 12 (1): 85–135.

Shakdiel, Leah. 2001. "Privatize and Rule: Is It Possible?" 9 Deot 5–6.

Schudson, Michael. 1999. "You've Got Mail: A Few Observations on Hope". *Social Research* 66: 625–628.

Segal, Dimitry. 1999. Endnote, in *How Much Land Does a Man Need? And Other Stories*, by Lev Tolstoy, 319–347. Jerusalem: Carmel. Hebrew.

Sexton, Shannon D. 1999. "A Custody System Free of Gender Preferences and Consistent with the Best Interests of the Child: Suggestions for a More Protective and Equitable Custody System". *Kentucky Law Journal* 88: 761–801.

Siegel, Deborah. 2013. "Open Adoption: Adoptive Parents' Reactions Two Decades Later". *Social Work* 58 (1): 43–52.

Siegel, Reva. 2004. "Equality Talk: Antisubordination and Anticlassification Values in Constitutional Struggles over Brown". *Harvard Law Review* 117: 1470–1547.

Silver, Marjorie A. 1999. "Love, Hate and Other Emotional Interference in the Lawyer–Client Relationship". *Clinical Law Review* 6: 259–313.

Sitbon, Ofter. 2008. "Editor's Comments First Action Ma'asei Mishpat". *Periodical on Law and Social Reform* 1: 11–15. Hebrew.

Slaughter, M. Malcolm. 2000. "Contested Identities: The Adoption of American Indian Children and the Liberal State". *Social and Legal Studies* 9: 227–248.

Slonim-Nevo, Vered and Itzhak Lander. 2008. *Stories We Tell Our Clients: Alleviating Suffering and Understanding Classic and Innovative Therapeutic Approaches*. Lyme Regis: Russell House Pub.

Smith, Carole. 1997. "Children's Rights: Judicial Ambivalence and Social Resistance". *International Journal of Law, Policy and the Family* 11: 103–139.

Smith, David James. 1995. *The Sleep of Reason: The James Bulger Case*. London: Arrow.

Steinsaltz, Adin. 2001. *Simple Words: Thinking about What Really Matters in Life*. New York: Simon and Schuster.

Stevenson, Olive. 1992. "Social Work Intervention to Protect Children: Aspects of Research and Practice". *Child Abuse Review* 1 (1): 19–32.

Stolle, Dennis P. 2000. Introduction, in *Practicing Therapeutic Jurisprudence: Law as a Helping Profession*, edited by Dennis Stolle, David Wexler and Bruce Winick, xv–xvii. Durham: Carolina Academic Press.

Suleiman, Susan Rubin. 1994. *Risking Who One is: Encounters with Contemporary Art and Literature*. Cambridge: Harvard University Press.

Sutherland, Elaine. 1999. *Child and Family Law*. Edinburgh: T and T Clark.

Tahmadebi-Birgani, Victoria. 2014. *Emmanuel Levinas and the Politics of Non-Violence*. Toronto: University of Toronto Press.

Tamir, Yael. 1993. *Liberal Nationalism*, Princeton: Princeton University Press.

Tannen, Deborah. 1999. *The Argument Culture: Stopping America's War of Words*. New York: Ballantine.

Taylor, Charls. 1991. *The Ethics of Authenticity*. Cambridge: Harvard University Press.

Taylor, Charles. 1994. "The Politics of Recognition", in *Multiculturalism: Examining the Politics of Recognition*, edited by Amy Gutmann, 25–73. Princeton: Princeton University Press.

Tolou-Shams, Marina, Wendy Hadley, Selby Conrad, and Larry Brown. 2012. "The Role of Family Affect in Juvenile Drug Court Offenders' Substance Use and HIV Risk". *Journal of Child and Family Studies* 21 (3): 449–456.

Twerski, Abraham J. 2000. *The Spiritual Self: Reflections on Recovery and God*. Center City: Hazelden.

Van Bueren, Geraldine. 1998a. "Opening Pandora's Box: Protecting Children Against Torture, Cruel, Inhuman and Degrading Treatment and Punishment", in *Childhood*

Abused: Protecting Children Against Torture, Cruel, Inhuman and Degrading Treatment and Punishment, edited by Geraldine Van Bueren, 57–74. Farnham: Ashgate.

Van Bueren, Geraldine. 1998b. *The International Rights of the Child*. Dordrecht: Kluwer Academic Publishers.

Van Praagh, Shauna. 1997. "Religion, Custody, and a Child's Identities". *Osgoode Hall Law Journal* 35: 309–378.

Van Praagh, Shauna. 1999a. "The Education of Religious Children: Families, Communities and Constitutions". *Buffalo Law Review* 47: 1343–1345.

Van Praagh, Shauna. 1999b. "Faith, Belonging, and the Protection of 'Our' Children". *Windsor Yearbook of Access to Justice Annual* 17: 154–203.

White, Michael. 2011. *Narrative Practice: Continuing the Conversations*. New York: Norton.

Walant, Karen B. 1995. *Creating the Capacity for Attachment: Treating the Addictions and the Alienated Self*. Lanham: Rowman and Littlefield.

Webster's Encyclopedic Unabridged Dictionary of the English Language. 1996. New Revised Edition. New York: Gramercy.

Weiner, Myron. 1991. *The Child and The State in India: Child Labor and Education Policy in Comparative Perspective*. Delhi: Oxford University Press.

Wexler, David. 2000. "Therapeutic Jurisprudence and the Culture of Critique", in *Practicing Therapeutic Jurisprudence Law as a Helping Profession*, edited by Dennis Stolle, David Wexler and Bruce Winick, 449–464. Durham: Carolina Academic Press.

Wilson, Sarah. 1997. "Identity, Genealogy, and the Social Family: The Case of Donor Insemination". *International Journal of Law, Policy, and the Family* 11: 281–282.

Winnicott, Donald. 1985. *Deprivation and Delinquency*, edited by Clare Winnicott, Ray Sheperd and Madeleine Davis. London: Taylor and Francis.

Woodhouse, Barbara Bennett. 1994. "Afterword: Deconstructing Solomon's Dilemma". Symposium: Solomon's Dilemma: Exploring Parental Rights. *Connecticut Law Review* 26: 1525–1532.

Wright, Nancy A. 1998. Welfare Reform Under the Personal Responsibility Act: Ending Welfare as We Know It or Governmental Child Abuse?" *Hastings Constitutional Law Quarterly* 25 (3): 357–420.

Zafran, Ruth. 2010. "Children's Rights as Relational Rights: The Case of Relocation". *American Journal of Gender 18 Social Policy and the Law*: 163–217.

Index

www.ingramcontent.com/pod-product-compliance
Lightning Source LLC
Chambersburg PA
CBHW031327230926
51848CB00001B/120
9789004223660